STANDING IN LINE

30 YEARS OF OBSESSIVE QUEUING AT WIMBLEDON

Ben Chatfield

with illustrations by Zebedee Helm

First published by Pitch Publishing, 2018

Pitch Publishing
A2 Yeoman Gate
Yeoman Way
Worthing
Sussex
BN13 3QZ
www.pitchpublishing.co.uk
info@pitchpublishing.co.uk

A CIP catalogue record is available for this book
from the British Library.

ISBN 978-1-78531-360-8

Typesetting and origination by Pitch Publishing
Printed in India by Replika Press

CONTENTS

An Introduction To The Book .9

The Complete Works Of The All England Lawn Tennis
   & Croquet Club (Abridged) 13

The Tennis Calendar And The 'Grand Slam' 17

The Basics. 21

Rufus The Hawk's-Eye View Of The Grounds 26

Mind Your Ps And Queues: How To Behave 27

25 June 2013 38

The Diary 1984–2013. 40

Wimbleballs. 48

How *Not* To Dress For Wimbledon (Part 1) 81

White Noise (Part 1) 100

White Noise (Part 2) 140

The Daily Smash. 159

The University Of (Queue) Life 181

Undercrackers 203

How *Not* To Dress For Wimbledon (Part 2) 212

When In Wombledon, Do As Wombles Do 234

Epilogue. 267

Outtakes 279

Read On. 281

In memory of Peter Doohan 1961–2017 282

Endnotes 284

For Victoria

I have spoken to Ben twice. Once on a tube train, and once on the phone in 2014, when he interviewed me about my match with Boris Becker in 1987, for which I had more than my 15 minutes of fame. On both occasions he struck me as strangely, almost unsettlingly, knowledgeable about my life and tennis career. But it is this attention to detail which made me want to read this, an almost alternative history to Wimbledon in the modern era, as these poor limeys searched desperately for a champion. Thank God they found Andy. Or else he might have never left me alone.

Peter Doohan, AKA 'The Becker Wrecker'
1961–2017

I have tried to recreate events, locales and conversations from my memories of them. In order to maintain their anonymity in some instances I have changed the names of individuals and places. I may have changed some identifying characteristics and details such as physical properties, occupations and places of residence.

A big thank you to Zebedee, for his great talent and also being an absolute joy to work with. Even when Aston Villa had been relegated.

With particular thanks to Jane and Paul Camillin at Pitch Publishing, for embracing and believing in the idea.

To the learned team at the Kenneth Ritchie Wimbledon Library for all their help over the years, most notably Robert McNicol and Audrey Snell. A special thank you to the late Alan Little, whose advice and knowledge over the years has been invaluable. To Alexandra Willis at the AELTC for her continued support of our work, as well as Shelley Blake and Sarah Frandsen.

A particular tip of the straw trilby for the Honorary Stewards, the wonderful group of people who make sure that pretty much everyone who visits the Wimbledon Queue goes home with a smile on their face.

A big nod to Matt Little, for connecting me in some small way to such life-changing events. Even if he seemed to try a lot harder conditioning Andy Murray than he did with me, aged 14.

And for my Mum, the original Queuer.

'I remember talking to Roy Emerson … I'll never forget him telling me, he says, "Billie, what keeps me going … when I'm at Wimbledon and I walk in and see all those people who've been up all night to see us, " he says, "We are so lucky," … and he's right.'

Billie Jean King[i]

AN INTRODUCTION TO THE BOOK

There are three strands to this short tome.

1.
I am fascinated by tennis

There is something in the basic, almost pugilistic, simplicity of the game that appeals to me like nothing else. It's best put by Harry Hopman, the legendary Australian, who said, 'The art of lawn tennis is control and restraint, and putting the ball where the other guy ain't.' As a boy I was also highly aware that our male players were not close to winning Wimbledon and for some reason it really bothered me. The British ladies had been more successful, with four of them[1] winning it since Fred Perry's last victory in 1936, but being a boy the craving instilled in me early on was for a Gentlemen's Champion. For this reason this is not a 30-year history of the tournament, it's a memoir, and one based on what was most memorable to me.

2.
I was born in Wimbledon

I grew up down the road in a slightly less leafy part, but I am, effectively, a local. I first arrived in Church Road with my Mum in June 1984, aged ten and a twelfth, staring open-mouthed and captivated as that giant green world unfurled in front of me. Even now, whilst I live within an overhit lob of Centre Court, I still sometimes get that feeling in my stomach. It's a feeling which says summer, tennis, glamour and the whole world coming here, to my own doorstep. It's like a massive film set, or global reality TV show, based right where I live. A reality show in which the best characters come back every year, if the viewers love, or, even better, loathe them. It is also never-ending due to the fact that ex-players are just as welcome, often reinventing themselves in the media

---

1 Dorothy Round, Angela Mortimer, Ann Jones, Virginia Wade.

and resurrecting their careers long after they've hung up their whites. It's a show which mixes the slightly prissy world of an English garden party, and its associated class barriers, with the brash and flash world of an international sport, rife with egos, sponsorship deals, image rights, glitz and cosmopolitan glamour. And for two weeks it takes over everything, sporting and otherwise.

For many it is a social and celebrity event as much as it is a sporting one. You only have to look at the attention paid, across all of the media, especially the BBC, as to who's got one of the 80 seats in the Royal Box each day. It's a bit like a nightclub, with the stars rocking up outside in their limos, cameras flashing as they step out, all 70s shades and lanyards. It even has bouncers. Well, stewards, but it's the same idea.

I especially love the newspaper coverage, with Wimbledon being the one thing which can truly unite all the titles in terms of the blanket fascination, in all kinds of frivolity. These days the popular reality shows are largely tabloid fodder but this SW19 fix is omnipresent, in all of the papers, as even the broadsheets indulge in a healthy dose of tennis tittle-tattle.

3.
The Queue

Like most people I don't really enjoy just standing in a line for hours on end. George Mikes, the Hungarian-born British journalist with a keen eye for sharp observation, said, 'An Englishman, even if he is alone, forms an orderly queue of one,'[ii] emphasising the point that everyone seems fixated on the British queuing obsession. But something happens in SW19 when you get in that very specific 'Queue'; it's the sense of what might be, what might happen, of stories not yet written. It is therefore fitting that the phrase, 'Good things come to those who wait', is traced back to Violet Fane, a British writer of the late 19th century, and early Queue visionary.

I would still love to have debenture tickets every day through some mad old aunt who owns half of Gloucestershire, but I don't, and nor do most people. So every year it all comes down to that Queue, that magnificently democratic Queue. That's how we can get access to a world of wonder. And everyone's invited.

So here you are, this is my love letter. In romantic terms I am Pygmalion; I have fallen in love with a kind of sculpture, in which Wimbledon is the artistic creation, the masterpiece. Or in modern parlance it's a bit like that woman who fell in love with the Eiffel Tower, or that bloke and his Ford Capri.

THE COMPLETE WORKS OF THE ALL ENGLAND LAWN TENNIS & CROQUET CLUB (ABRIDGED)

OR

'EVERYTHING YOU NEED TO KNOW ABOUT WIMBLEDON IN UNDER FOUR MINUTES'

In 1874 Major Walter Wingfield invented a game he snappily called 'Sphairistiké'. The word appeared to blend Norwegian with the French past historic and literally no one, even the greatest linguists, could say it. It was replaced with 'Lawn Tennis', possibly from the French word *tenez* ('hold', or 'take it'), which caught on like eating strawberries with cream. The game-for-a-laugh Victorians completely embraced the concept, so much so that when the first Championships were held at Worple Road in 1877, the players actually paid to enter[2]. In 1908 the Olympic tennis was held there, Brits winning golds in pretty much all events and crowds were turning up in their thousands.

The 1920s saw the era of elegant French lady Suzanne Lenglen, who dressed like a supermodel, waltzed around like Greta Garbo and smashed down sexual barriers with the same venom she used to hit her forehand, winning the event six times. Next up, having outgrown its grounds, the Club headed up the hill, through the village and on to the new site at Church Road. Booming public interest saw a ballot introduced for tickets, a system destined to both delight and frustrate for the next hundred years.

The 1930s were all about the gallant British working-class hero, Fred Perry, who won it three times, and by the

---

2   You can still see the site, near the high street, which is now the playing fields for Wimbledon High School.

end of the decade the lawns were being shown on newfangled 'television' for the first time. The Second World War saw Centre Court bombed, meaning no tournament for five years and parts of the Club ploughed in to a farm, complete with livestock. After war inconveniently interrupted play, order was restored in the 40s, with the gentlemen's trousers a lot shorter, as were the ladies' dresses.

The cool, jazzy 1950s saw the world start groovin', a point proved by the fact that all the players in the draw received commemorative ashtrays to celebrate the Coronation. The 1960s saw the dominance of brilliant Australian Rod Laver (amongst a plethora of brilliant Australians in general) and the first 'Open' Wimbledon, at which professionals first competed alongside amateurs for the big prizes. The 1970s witnessed a big players' strike (surprisingly not started by the French), the rise of the trailblazing Billie Jean King and the first black man, an all-round suave dude called Arthur Ashe, winning the title. We also had a British winner in the Ladies, Virginia Wade, and the Queen made a rare visit for her Silver Jubilee to hand her the prize. The same success was not shared by the British men, who appeared to be getting progressively worse.

By the late 70s, unlike music, tennis entered a golden era, and a massive boom time in the US, with the rock star looks of Björn Borg and the combined incendiary force of John McEnroe and Jimmy Connors, who took the sport to a new level of pop culture significance. The importance of this 70s-80s era cannot be overplayed – tennis went berserk, from effete to offensive – and did much to shape the fiercely competitive game as we know it today.

The women, led by Billie Jean, Martina Navratilova and Chrissie Evert, staged their own cultural revolution, just without the rude hand gestures and rows with the crowd/ umpires/each other/anyone who looked at them funny, as they took the game to new heights of athleticism and competition. Next up was Boris Becker, throwing himself around the court like a child on a sugar rush, crowds of over half a million, then Andre Agassi with his revolutionary take on apparel (cycling shorts, bad hair) and, in 1997, equal prize money awarded for men and women. A cheeky streaker took the roof, and her clothes, off, then the Club put a new one on Centre, the astonishing Williams sisters from California emerged to transform the women's game and we all witnessed the extraordinary rebirth of McEnroe as a jovial, witty, tongue-often-in-cheek TV pundit/commentator *sans pareil*.

Recent years have seen a ~~rubbish~~ proper movie all about the tournament, the players embracing a return to the politeness of the 60s, sporting and professional jumps in the game making it almost unrecognisable from that played even 25 years ago and an elegant man who played tennis as if he was being soundtracked by a symphony orchestra sweeping through Beethoven's Fifth. We had a _very_ long match, two Queues merging in to one and another 'golden era', which coined the term 'Big 4' for Roger, Rafa, Novak and Andy. To be fair it was initially more of a 'Big 3 and a bit' but then, finally, after 77 years, or 28,105 days, or 76 outbreaks of collective headscratching, or 40-something million minutes, we saw a British winner of the men's singles title.

The End.

THE TENNIS CALENDAR AND THE 'GRAND SLAM'

People often refer to the major tennis tournaments as 'Grand Slams', which is technically incorrect, in that they should really be called 'Majors'. There are four major tennis tournaments, at which the men's and women's events are played simultaneously, which all carry the most ranking points; the Australian Open in Melbourne, the French Open in Paris, Wimbledon in Wimbledon and the US Open in New York.

These are the 'Majors', even if the whole world, possibly with the exception of me, now calls them 'Grand Slams'. The four of these major tournaments together were called a 'Grand Slam', in the sense that if you win all the Majors (in any event, including doubles) in one calendar year then you have achieved the Grand Slam. It is kind of a big deal to do this in the singles discipline. It was achieved by Don Budge

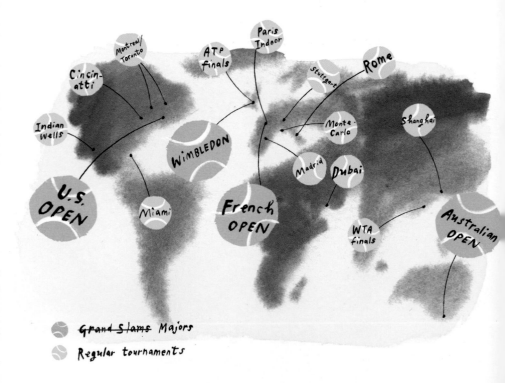

Grand Slams Majors

Regular tournaments

in 1938, Maureen Connolly in 1953, Rod Laver in 1962 and 1969 (the only person to do it twice, the second time even more incredible than the first), Margaret Court in 1970 and Steffi Graf in 1988 (who also added the Olympics gold for good measure).

Scattered around the rest of these Majors are pretty big events all over the world – some are only for ladies, like Stuttgart, and some only the gents, like Monte Carlo, which seems like a rough deal for the ladies. The term 'Grand Slam' itself most likely dates back to playing card games, with golf also using it in the same way as far back as 1930. Despite their utter brilliance, the mythical Grand Slam has been a feat never achieved by Martina Navratilova, Pete Sampras, Serena Williams or Roger Federer.

It should be noted here that Wimbledon is the only Major at which you can get tickets for showcourts by sleeping out the night before.

I have come to see this as a mixed blessing.

'People line the road and wave, and it's all sunlight and lawns. At the dressing-room entrance you step out, carrying a stack of rackets, and listen to the people whispering. Wherever you go, they whisper … The dressing-rooms are stocked with Robinson's fruit juices, and the showers deliver steaming torrents. Up in the restaurant there are hot meals, and in the little lounge, desks with All England writing paper. Very upstage is Wimbledon … the members stand about in large hats and eat strawberries. Everybody seems to be patient; just standing there, and pleased to be around.'

Gordon Forbes, *A Handful of Summers*[v]

THE BASICS

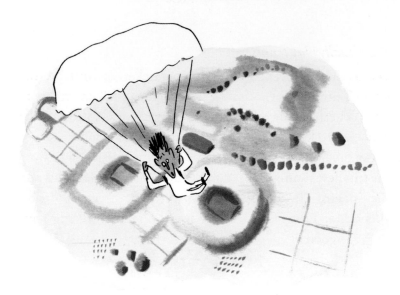

There are six ways to get into Wimbledon, without the use of parachutes:

1

You send a self-addressed envelope to the AELTC before Christmas and they pull all the names out of a ballot from March onwards, excluding yours[3].

I have done this every year, for 26 years, and have received tickets precisely once, when I got two tickets for the second Wednesday on Centre Court, men's quarter-finals, probably my favourite day of the tournament. This was also the first day of my honeymoon in Sicily.

The process is mainly notable for people you know, who know nothing about tennis, saying things like, 'Oh my God, I got men's semi-finals day tickets in the ballot. Is that good? *And* it's the first time I have tried!' Once I even had someone ask, 'Do the people attending also have to dress predominantly in white?' I obviously said they did.

---

3   Bitterness around this subject is a recurrent theme.

2

You actually play tennis.

Tennis clubs all over the UK get given tickets by the LTA (the Lawn Tennis Association) to ballot out to their members to buy. Whether this qualifies you for an appreciation of the game at pro level I can't say, but I suppose it just about seems reasonable. I have heard stories of groups of friends finding the smallest tennis clubs in the country in the Hebrides and then paying the annual fee just so they can get the ticket allocation. This is the kind of smart lateral thinking I am not very good at.

3

You buy them from ticket websites.

Every day the AELTC put 500 tickets for each showcourt on the Ticketmaster website, but you will need a Bletchley Park-level cryptanalyst code breaker to get near them and I have literally never heard of anyone, ever, managing to get hold of any this way. Otherwise it's other ticket sales sites which offer resold debenture tickets to anyone, but for that you are looking at £800 each which, however you cut it, is the same price as a second-hand Jaguar.

4

You buy them from ticket touts.

I am not aghast at the concept of people selling things, in a broader sense, it's just that touts can be very annoying. People approach tout interactions with the same wariness normally reserved for charity clipboard merchants, when it seems to follow the same principle as buying anything that someone else has, which you want, and are willing to pay over the odds for.

It's like selling a rare old record at a car boot sale for an inflated price – if you don't want to pay the inflated price, don't. It's just that the touts are, almost always, massive rotters who look like humanised weasels, who would definitely fleece you, so you should avoid it. Illegally bought tickets can often be spotted so you might also end up getting arrested, which is not what you probably want from a summer's day out. Sometimes silly people ignore this counsel and then blub when they get turned away at the gate for having a hooky ticket. These are the kinds of people who live in villages and go round saying how 'No one locks their front doors where we live' and then get burgled.

5

You are filthy rich and know other filthy rich people who make your life a non-filthy cakewalk. Not just for Wimbledon debenture tickets, but in general.

In the gospel truth words of Matthew (Chapter 13: Verse 12), 'Whoever has will be given more, and they will have an abundance.' He adds, getting on a roll now, and clearly talking about the Queuers, 'Whoever does not have, even what they have will be taken from them.' Often by the rain.

6

You queue up.

This used to be a case of rocking up to the street pavement outside the museum about midnight on the night before with a camp bed, some plastic sheeting, fish and chips and an alarm clock, to get your pick of tickets for Centre or No.1 Court. Stewards would come down the line giving out punnets of strawberries and cream for free and the tournament always seemed to be timed with England making the semi-finals of major football tournaments[4], as the country bathed in glorious, endless sunshine.

By the time of writing you need to realistically queue for a full day and night to guarantee a ticket of choice and The Queue itself is now a Glastonbury-inspired makeshift holiday camp in a park down the road. It can be such a punishing ordeal that once you are in line you actually get given a sticker (in the same way as people completing the London Marathon get a silver cape) saying 'I've queued at Wimbledon', a veritable badge of honour. It can also be the most joyfully weird and wonderful way to spend a sunny day in London, effectively camping for free in a lovely green park, full of other people in a really good mood, who also tend to know a fair bit about the wonderful game of tennis. And we really shouldn't moan, no other Major tournaments organise anything like it, and it's also a massive improvement on sleeping on the pavement. It just makes it all a bit more pleasant, so more people do it, so it makes it harder for me to get tickets.

---

4 This has only happened twice since 1966.

RUFUS THE HAWK'S-EYE VIEW OF THE GROUNDS

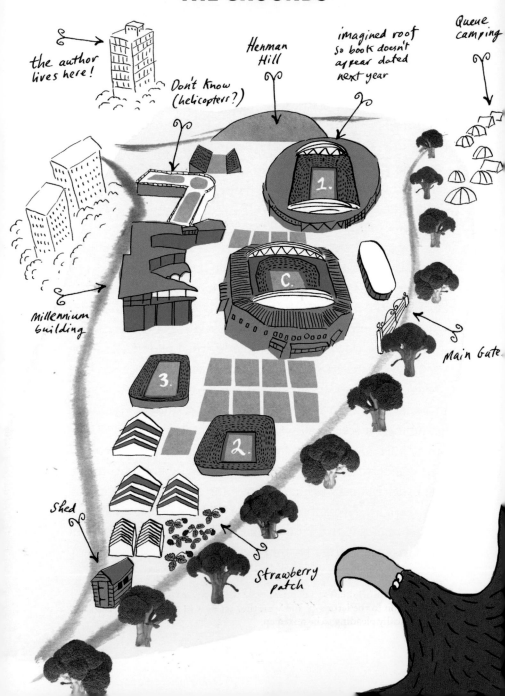

MIND YOUR PS AND QUEUES[5]: HOW TO BEHAVE

---

5 The phrase originates from printing, in which typesetters had to pay careful attention to the letters 'p' and 'q' as they sat next to each other on the rack, practically pleading to be mixed up.

1. Queuing

The *Oxford English Dictionary* defines a queue as, 'a line or sequence of people or vehicles awaiting their turn to be attended to or to proceed.' Keen Brit appraiser, George Mikes, observed that, 'Where other nationalities mass frenziedly, the British queue,' a quote also referenced in *Debrett's A-Z of Modern Manners[iii]*. The phenomenon is apparently linked back to world wars and rationing, emotionally feeding a desire to catch up with the community you lived in. Mikes goes on to say, 'Queuing is the national passion of an otherwise dispassionate race. The English are rather shy about it, and deny that they adore it.' This seems a little extreme, but perhaps this book is not the best place to start trying to disprove the allegation.

The overall concept of organised queuing in the modern era is an interesting one in itself, with the science and slightly dark arts applied to the Disneyland queue paving the way when it opened in 1955. This was primarily based on the discovery that people would behave a lot better if you told them what they were in for; 'YOUR WAIT TIME IS 6 HOURS FROM THIS POINT'. The whole concept of queuing outdoors for entertainment was relatively new and the mass crowds Disneyland was attracting meant that the 'Imagineers'[6] had to think fast. Far-out art installations and blokes dressed as rainbows kept the crowds distracted, before the launch of actual pre-shows and in-queue entertainment. As writer Ranjani Iyer Mohanty, an experienced and patient queuer, explains in the *New York Times*:

> 'A 1969 paper by Harvard professor Leon Mann argued that queues are a "miniature social system". Richard Larson of M.I.T. took it further, stating that, in order to function, a queue must be fair: It must follow the rule of FIFO — first-in, first-out. People must be served in the order they are lined up in; otherwise, the result can be queue rage. Queues also have a profound philosophical aspect. The logic of the line, and not just in France, is liberté, égalité, fraternité. It translates like this: We are free to run around like chickens with our heads cut off, but if we behave in a brotherly/sisterly/neighbourly manner and queue up, we all have an equal chance of getting in. As Descartes may have put it, "We queue, therefore we are."'

This fact is backed up in The Championships' own *A Guide To Queuing* pamphlet which states that, 'The operation of The Queue, for on-day ticket sales at The Championships, has been designed to ensure fairness.' Even George Mikes agrees, stating, 'A man in a queue is a fair man ... the image of a true Briton.' As the idea of watching lawn tennis on a summer's day is a popular one it follows that queuing at Wimbledon has always been a major part of the experience, and one which many enjoy almost as much as the sporty bit. Descartes, the 17th century French Boffin, or 'Bauphin', Extraordinaire is, therefore, my guiding light, he is the All

---

6   The Disney take on designers and engineers, the loons.

Knowing King of Kings, a deity and a demigod, he is the Father of the Wimbledon Ticketless. I Queue, therefore I am Descartian.

2. Meritocracy

Tennis is often, wrongfully in my mind, accused of being a bit elitist, or exclusive. It's not really, it's certainly easier to get involved with it if you are stinking rich, but so are most things.

To me, the game itself has always had a certain merito-cratic magic on court, for in tennis the best player almost always wins. You can't really 'nick' a game of tennis, like you can score a last-minute winner in football, having been consummately outplayed for 90 minutes. There is a winner, and that winner is almost always the deserved one. You need the mental toughness to get over the line, to finish it, which is why the final game of Andy Murray v Novak Djokovic in the 2013 final was so astonishingly tense. Murray had held, and lost, three consecutive Championship points and Djokovic was, in the astute words of the BBC's Jonathan Overend, 'grinning like a Bond villain'. Murray, even then, cock-a-hoop at two sets to love up, might have blown his chance. The finishing line cares not for momentum in tennis, you can trip on your face within a metre of it. Just ask the late, great Jana Novotna.

The Queue at Wimbledon is the best, and worst, of tennis, but not always as fair. In one sense it is a wonderfully simple system; you get there first, you are in front of me; you set your alarm earlier, you deserve it, you went the extra mile. It's FIFO in full effect. But it can also make you crawl on your hands and knees (in some cases literally) to get anywhere. It can, with the help of The Weather, slap you in the face without so much as a (storm) warning, leaving you with nothing. This all results in a love/grate relationship with The Queue, and therefore The Championships[7].

More often than not I find myself wondering why I keep loving something which doesn't always love me back, which never rewards me with a ballot ticket, which forces me to wait in line, which pushes my patience to the limit, like an aloof unrequited love, destined to spurn me.

3. Expectations

If you win the wrestle with The Queue and actually manage to get A Ticket you pass through a turnstile after which you are held in something approaching a giant farmyard pen, but without the feeding troughs. Security staff create a physical wall and, at 10.30am, they walk the crowd in to the grounds, like a human wave, allowing you to disperse calmly in to the nooks and crannies of the whole All England Club. This moment is highly exciting.

Once set free in the stadium you will generally get to see three or four matches, which is kind of a better deal than, say, going to the football where you get two 45-minute halves. In addition to this, the tickets allocated to The Overnight Queuers are some of the best in the stadium, not up in the Gods or behind a concrete pillar. In bumper years you might, as I did in 1993, get two epic five-setters starring historically significant players at the peak of their powers.

But by the same measure you might queue up all day and all night and see jack squat. Nothing. It could rain almost all day and you'll get to see no tennis at all. Maybe a bit of a refund if you're lucky, or maybe the option of the same ticket for next year? And that's not enough, because no one can prepare you for the hideousness that is queuing

---

7   If the employment of capitals is getting annoying then you are going to have to get used to it. Wimbledon Love 'Em.

up in the rain, in a park in south London. On your own. On a Tuesday.

4. *The Weather*

There is of course an overall obsession in the United Kingdom with the weather; we are actually a Kingdom United by our obsession with The Weather. This often strikes foreign people as funny as our climate is generally atrocious, making it completely ok for anyone in the world to poke fun at us about the overall dreariness, apart from Parisians. Parisians have worse weather than us, but act like they live in the Mediterranean, which is plain, well, plain Parisian.

Meteorological obsession reaches a peak in the summer, largely because we don't very often have balmy summer days in which you can actually stand around outside in the evening, so, when we do experience this, everyone embraces it like it's the first time it has ever happened. In short, when it is warm, us Brits go a bit loopy. It's really worth seeing, everybody goes to the pub every night after work and stands around chatting, acting as if having four large glasses of rosé on an empty stomach is in no way making them barely able to stand up. Women otherwise scared of showing their ankles start sunbathing in the park in their underwear. Every single house with access to open space starts to barbecue their food like it's the Age of Pithecanthropus and pull the telly out on an extension lead so they can sunbathe while ~~drinking themselves blind~~ watching the tennis.

Children roam the streets on BMXs like feral futuristic KidCops while their parents are passed out on sun loungers in the garden at 8pm. Commercial radio stations play the full seven-minute version of The Isley Brothers' 'Summer Breeze' about six times a day and every single newsagent rations ice lollies. It's incredible. It's like there's a war on or something. If you then combine hot weather with the gargantuan event that is the world's biggest tennis tournament then you're really in for it. Hence the weather obsession reaching, yep, boiling point, for these two weeks.

For those of you who like to know the ending of a book before you read it (in case you die, like Harry in *When Harry Met Sally*) I should also point out here that normally it rains quite a bit at Wimbledon and normally all our players (especially the fellas) get knocked out in the first round. But sometimes in life (the spoiler alert) it is a scorcher for Finals' weekend and the opposite of this happens.

5. Jingoism

Jingoism sounds like a nice thing, what with many words ending in '–ingo' being quite fun and playful; Ringo, bingo, Renault Twingo. It is in reality a posh way of saying 'loves a Union Jack', or 'extremely patriotic' or 'likes a bit of a war

with people that don't look like them'. Whilst an individual sport, The Championships can also bring out the partisan in the garden party as old national rivalries can rise to the fore[8], only exaggerated when the crowd get a bit oiled. It should also be noted that, like the Olympics, it's all about Great Britain in tennis and not just England. For this we should be eternally grateful, and it will become very significant later on, in around 2013.

Great Britain was, from just after the time of dashing Roger Taylor in the early 1970s (he was dishy enough to make grown women faint), going through what one might call a 'fallow period' in the Gentlemen's Singles. Mark Cox and Buster Mottram floated around in the 20-something rankings in the world throughout the 70s, but never really won anything. John Lloyd looked the part, and would have the perfect wife to fulfil tennis promise, but, after getting to the final of a depleted Australian Open, he didn't cause much trouble at the big events.

---

8   The USA v Russia … Germany v Great Britain/France/Holland/Russia/ Poland …. Switzerland v Nobody.

This is why Timothy Henry Henman was greeted with such delight. When he got kicked out in 1995 for a controversy involving a ball girl I initially thought we had some kind of Home Counties' Georgie Best on our hands. Not so, but his achievements in getting to world No. 4 are often overlooked based on the player who came immediately after him, and his significance in the story of British tennis cannot be overstated.

The writer Simon Barnes described his repeated near-misses at Wimbledon as being 'part of the rhythm of national life', and, as a nation, we love a near miss, the nearer the better. I will always remember him for a seemingly endless stream of evening matches on Centre Court, in the latter stages of the tournament, in which he gave the entire nation the collywobbles en masse as we ate our tea. A guy who could go head to head with the Big Guns, and within a whisker of a Wimbledon final (four times), served to reawaken my own lapsed love of the game in that period.

Added to this there was a joy to 'supporting' Great Britain at tennis, unlike supporting 'Eng-ger-land' at football. At tennis we could be the underdog, it was fun and no one really cared if we lost.

At football we always expected to win, despite the fact that we never did, it was the very opposite of fun and the country went into national mourning when we lost. Every year for Wimbledon the papers would amusingly feature some kind of chart showing how the Brits were all out ... and it was only quarter to three on the first Tuesday. This had the knock-on effect of allowing us all to focus on our favourites from the international pantheon of glamorous international stars and actually enjoy it all rather than have to 'care' too much.

6. 'The Fortnight'

The British also have an extremely strange relationship with tennis. Unlike in France it really is not our national summer sport, it's barely played in schools and cricket, with its team dynamic (and more regular successes), has always seemed closer to the British heart than the loneliness of the non-Major-winning tennis star. But Wimbledon seems to bring out something entirely different, something everyone feels qualified to talk about, however little they may actually follow the sport outside of these two weeks. In most cases this is not at all, but if you are in England over The Fortnight (as some people like to refer to Wimbledon) you might think that we talk about absolutely Nothing Else. This is also displayed in statistical form as you can pick up any publication during the First Week and find an article telling you that the tournament uses seven tons of topsoil, 58 million grass seeds, 57,000 tennis balls, serves 166,000 bowls of strawberries, 320,000 glasses of Pimms and if you took out all the ball boys' and ball girls' shoelaces and laid them end to end you'd get to the moon and back three times.

7. Obsession

Noun *1. the domination of one's thoughts or feelings by a persistent idea, image, desire.*
Every year around May I start gearing up for the inevitable. Inevitably I won't have won tickets in the ballot and so, like a lemming, I start to run towards the edge of the cliff that is The Queuing. The desire and persistence of that feeling is unavoidable and intractable and totally dominates my thinking as I become obsessed. It is the Charge of the Light Brigade. I start to gallop towards the inevitable trauma that is the standing in line. This is combined with the largely farcical idea that a British man might actually win it and the

even more farcical idea that my personal physical presence is somehow linked to that happening.

The Queue will constantly ask you the same questions: How far are you willing to go? How long is too long? When is it too much? How much time is too much time off work? Can you get wetter than 'wet'? Why do you always buy those camping chairs with the drinks holder in the sale for £10.99 when you know they will break within an hour?

I know the desire in me is too strong to resist. What might happen? What if a Brit ... What might have been if I was there? What if I miss a classic because I sat on my bum and watched it on the telly? This really is the crux of it all, the idea of missing out on something of global significance which is happening right on my doorstep. My obsession is therefore best described in the words of the 19th-century American writer, John Greenleaf Whittier, who summed it all up best when he wrote, 'Of all sad words of tongue or pen, the saddest are these, *"It might have been"*.'

25 JUNE 2013: BRITISH MEN'S WIMBLEDON DROUGHT REACHES 77th YEAR

At 5.30am the polite-sounding gentleman with the voice of J.R. Hartley[iv], wearing freshly laundered chinos, gently taps his umbrella on my tent door:

'Up and at em!' he suggests, as if we are about to charge across a foreign battlefield. In any normal walk of life this would be an enormous wind-up.

I order a breakfast bap from one of the stalls in the Merton Council refreshment set-up, over by the train tracks. What I receive, in exchange for £5, is a foamy burger bun filled with barely cooked, flaccid pork 'meat' and so much flabby rind that I feel like I am eating a fistful of elastic bands. I pack my tent away and take it over to the left luggage hut where two head girl-types from Wimbledon Girls' School bounce all over my early morning slumber like a couple of overly eager labrador puppies.

'Will it just be the tent and the eiderdown?!!' one joyfully roars at a volume level wildly inappropriate for this time of the morning/night. The other laughs riotously at nothing in particular and flicks her leonine mane of hair in time. 'And it's a sleeping bag, not an eiderdown,' I grumpily mutter, to myself.

On walking back to the silently throbbing mass of stirring human existence on that marshy field I am reminded of a Spencer Tunick art installation, a rising heap of anthropomorphic body heat, as the damp day breaks. But this time we are all wearing cagoules, and not stark naked.

Behind me is a man from Korea who is staring intently into the distance, as if he knows something terrible is coming, and the rest of us don't. In front of me are three women from Bromley who are all dressed as if they are in a beach bar in Kefalonia at 2pm in July. They have already started drinking white wine. It's 5.45am, raining and feels about minus 3°C.

I learned that they got up at 2.30am to get here and were dropped off by Claire's fiancé[9].

In The Queue I am not A Character. I am not flag-happy. Or dressed as a strawberry. I am just waiting. I tend to keep my head down, I withdraw in to myself. Sometimes this can lead to the early stages of self-absorption, then the devouring of one's own personality and finally the feeling of one's ego collapsing. This stems from a form of shyness, as opposed to a lack of sociability or mild sociopathy. On the right day I can actually be a veritable chatterbox, exchanging anecdotes, hosting impromptu gatherings in front of my tent and sharing my experience with Queue Newcomers. But you must never forget that you can be standing in That Queue for the best part of a day, and once you've opened those conversational floodgates there is no going back.

At about 6.10am the grey clouds crack open and a shaft of sunlight shoots through, lighting up the gloomy park. There is a spontaneous cheer from the thousands now present. I feel an overwhelming sense of pure joy.

---

9 By 8.45 Claire, the heaviest of the three drinkers, would be quietly escorted from The Queue and in to a First Aid tent, suffering from extreme cold, difficulty walking and the early stages of alcohol poisoning.

THE DIARY
1984-2013

LOVE AT FIRST SIGHT

My introduction to the joys of Wimbledon queuing came on Wednesday, 27 June 1984, aged ten. The year had been exciting already, what with Sweden winning the Eurovision Song Contest with a number called 'Diggi-Loo Diggi-Ley' and WHAM! releasing 'Wake Me Up Before you Go-Go'. My Mum picked me up at 12.15pm on a half-day and we walked to the bus stop, via the newsagents where I was allowed a blue raspberry-flavoured Mr Freeze ice pop[10]. It was, as in all the best childhood memories, wonderfully sunny and warm, and most likely a slightly idealised reconstruction.

At Wimbledon train station in the high street we hopped on to an old Routemaster bus emblazoned with the thrilling sign, 'TO & FROM WIMBLEDON TENNIS', taking our seats at the front of the upper deck. Once full, the bus took us up the hill, through the village and down Church Road where the glory of the All England Club is first seen, unfurling in front of you like a dream. The Queue seemed endless, just as it always would.

---

10 In the Eighties raspberry-flavoured iced treats (see also Slush Puppie) were always blue. I assume this is because red had already been bagged by the A-List strawberry.

STAR-SPANGLED

It was a wonderful parade of international people, all in one place, unlike anything I had ever seen. There weren't many Japanese people where I lived in south London, but here they were all around, along with Australians, Indians and exotic South Americans. I remember the north Americans most vividly, as, being aged ten, the USA seemed impossibly cool and aspirational, with television dominated by *Chips*, *The Dukes of Hazzard* and *The Fall Guy*. Those shows had a different look on the screen, a whole different colour palette, making America seem incredibly 'other', like a hazy distant planet. It was a place where seemingly everyone was tanned, had great hair and wore amazing white Nike trainers, knee socks and tiny jean shorts. And that was just the fellas. At the head of that line were the adversarial Glimmer Twins of world tennis; JP McEnroe and JS Connors, and I, like most people I knew, was firmly in the McEnroe camp. His wretched genius was less appreciated than his compulsive winning and his supercool Sergio Tacchini kit. Added to that, he argued with the adults about <u>everything</u>, something a ten-year-old could really relate to.

MAKING HIS MIND UP

John Lloyd was the top British player, ranked 31 that year, and he lost in straight sets in the third round to an American, Scott Davis. This was an inconvenience as he had stated his intent in the papers at the start of the week, under the declarative headline 'It's NOW or NEVER'[vi]. Lloyd never really got on with Wimbledon on a performance level but what he lacked in results he more than made up for in glitz, looking like one of the blokes in Bucks Fizz and being married to Chris Evert in her glamorous, 'primary-school-teacher-you've-got-a-crush-on' phase, one half of tennis' Golden Couple. I heard later that some people referred to him as 'Mr Evert' behind his back, which was a bit cruel, but she had won 16 Majors by that point to his none.

MUM, WE'RE NOT IN SOUTH LONDON ANYMORE

That day we walked along Church Road, through the teeming crowds, at every gate getting a glimpse of the action going on inside, as we looped into Somerset Road, eventually reaching the end and joining The Queue for 'ground passes'[11]. The main thing I remember about The Queue that day was that it seemed to take forever to move and a kindly man in clothes like I wore to school (funny hat, blazer, white shirt, tie) came along and gave me a bowl of strawberries and cream for no reason. He told me his name was David Jenkins and I called him 'Mr Jenkins', as back then us kids always spoke to adults with a respectful formality. 'Move along now, no dilly-dallying please,' I remember him politely barking at The Queue in general.

The mass of people crawled along as, thrillingly, you could now hear the sound of balls being thwacked, interspersed by oohs and aahs on what was then Court 2, next to the fence. At some point we entered through a turnstile and I was given a pristine white ticket, priced at £4.00, giving access to a pulsating world of festivity and delight. Wandering through the enormous maze that is the 'outside courts' I can vividly remember the overwhelming spectacle, as giants of the athletic arena, bronzed sporting gods and goddesses, did battle in immaculate grass arenas. But we were on a mission, and ten minutes later we had found it.

Another queue.

---

11 A non-showcourt ticket which entitles you to use unreserved seating and standing room on Courts No.3–18.

This one was for 'returned tickets' and appeared way longer than The Queue we had just left. Mum, who seemed to know what she was doing, assured me that all was in hand but it felt to me that, on arriving at the Holy Grail, we had now wilfully left and joined another group of people standing in a line and not watching tennis. These returned tickets were gathered up from red boxes situated by the exits where they had been handed in by (crazy) people actually leaving the stadium before the tennis had finished. This queue moved faster and in what seemed no time I was being dragged back through the crowds, in the direction whence we had come, past some stewards, under a few tunnels, down some walkways and boom, there it was.

Another queue.

My audible exasperation was met with a scowl from a giant soldier as it was clear that silence was very much in order in this cool corridor we were now standing in. Minutes later the sound of clapping erupted and we were heading up some stairs and in to the glorious daylight. We were here, on the Centre Court, and I could barely believe my eyes. It was like the moment in *The Wizard of Oz* when everything goes Technicolor.

THE BIG SMOKE

I already thought that a sports programme of any description was a thrill, particularly for football matches, of which I had a collection of hundreds, almost all from lower league games I had not attended. The giant official Wimbledon programme was handed to me by an Honorary Steward, who came over to where we were sitting. I can remember the adverts for 'The Virginia Slims World Championships', the 'Benson & Hedges Championships' and even Marlboro Leisure Wear.[12]

---

12 This was also an era when Martina Navratilova wore an entire kit sponsored by KIM cigarettes and Arthur Ashe was a spokesman for Philip Morris.

The steward told me that the programme was for me to keep and said, 'Toodle pip' when he left to go and talk to someone else. I was hooked by this stuff. I was even more hooked by the fact that we had seats to watch none other than J.P. McEnroe, playing doubles with Peter Fleming, against a pairing I had never heard of. This was definitely the most exciting thing that had happened to me since I fell out of the back door of the Ford Escort in the Safeways car park in 1982.

THE GLOBAL VILLAGE

On leaving the hallowed Centre Court I saw that play was still going on all over the place. My patient Mum was dragged from corner to corner as I devoured every last drop of tennis available, even as courts were covered with giant tents and the day drew in. We walked up the Church Road hill that evening, me walking backwards so I could keep looking at the grounds, until the view disappeared as we reached the road into Wimbledon village. It was a giant party and everyone was queuing … for everything! There were people standing in line at wooden bars, at tables selling t-shirts, at taxi stands and at streetside barbecues, it was like opening a door to a whole new life, all this queuing, and I seriously wanted to take my place.

THE TWILIGHT ZONE

We always watched *Wimbledon '84* on the telly at home and I was quite taken with a guy just six years older, and 40 kilos heavier, than me, called 'Boris' who seemed to spend as much time diving on the grass as he did hitting the ball. I decided straight away that he was to be 'my player'. It was also the Centenary year for the Ladies' Championships and on the Saturday the final was played out fittingly between Chris Lloyd (still listed then as 'Mrs J.M. Lloyd', after her husband) and Miss M. Navratilova, as it seemed to be every year. Chris Evert-Lloyd (as we all knew her) was the one my Dad said had nice legs, and I didn't have a clue what to make of Martina.

McEnroe destroyed Jimmy Connors to win the Gentlemen's Singles title the following day, 6-1, 6-1, 6-2, making just three unforced errors in the entire match[13]. Much later I would read that he was, that afternoon, in what sportsmen call 'the zone', a rarely reached dreamlike status of perfection in which everything becomes astonishingly easy and errors virtually disappear as a concept. He said afterwards that he was 'seeing the ball like a basketball', which I still think sounds pretty odd, and strangely more difficult.

---

13 It would be just one of a whopping 84 matches he won in 1984, losing only three.

Ladies' Champion *Martina Navratilova*
Gentlemen's Champion *John McEnroe*

WIMBLEBALLS
Wimbledon's funniest 'Colemanballs'

'Strawberries, cream and champers flowed like hot cakes.'
BBC RADIO 2

'Steffi has a tremendous presence when you're standing right next to her.'
VIRGINIA WADE

'The Gullikson twins here. An interesting pair – both from Wisconsin.'
DAN MASKELL

'These ball boys are marvellous. You don't even notice them. There's a left-handed one over there. I noticed him earlier.'
MAX ROBERTSON

'I had a feeling today that Venus Williams would either win or lose.'
MARTINA NAVRATILOVA

'Henman and Coria have met three times in the past and they've won one apiece.'
ANNABEL CROFT

'Andy Murray: the last British man in the men's or women's draw.'
JOHN INVERDALE

'I'm currently writing a screenplay that I haven't started yet.'
SERENA WILLIAMS

'In tennis there has to be a winner sometimes.'
ROGER FEDERER

'Laura Robson has just made the best possible start to her professional tennis career, she won the first set and lost the next two and is out.'
MARK POUGATCH

And the greatest of all time …

'I brought two hundred (headbands) with me and I've already given away about a hundred. I have no idea how many I have left.'
PAT CASH, 1988

With thanks to the 'Colemanballs' series, collated by Private Eye

FAIL TO PREPARE, PREPARE TO FAIL

After waiting 367 days for my second visit to Wimbledon, I planned for the booked Friday trip by laying out my kit before bed; knee-length Nike socks, a five-sizes-too-big Fred Perry polo (hand-me-down) and a brand new Olympus Sport headband/sweatband set, having saved up and bought these with my pocket money. A kind of McEnroe-inspired look, rendered largely cosmetic by the fact that it would be four years before I actually started to sweat. Sports fashion was a really big deal at primary school, with the spenny Italian brands like Ellesse, FILA, Diadora and Sergio Tacchini earning the highest playground respect. The pristine Lacoste whites of Frenchie Henri Leconte were also beginning to register on my radar, but I especially liked how he sometimes pretended he was blind when he missed a sitter, using his racket like a white stick and feeling for the lines. Looking back it was quite offensive.

IT NEVER RAINS, IT POURS

The first week in 1985 had been patchy and it was rumoured that lightning had actually struck Centre Court on the

Tuesday as biblical rains poured down[14]. In hindsight it was good to get my first experience of rain in The Queue, otherwise I may have been ill-prepared for the harrowing and traumatic years to come. On that Tuesday it turned on my dream in a way I would find it hard to forgive as, much like an English seaside resort on a wet Bank Holiday, I saw how the All England Club could move effortlessly from my own version of Disneyland to the 'Dreariest Place In England Where There is Nothing To Do But Mope'. Like a kind of post-apocalyptic horror movie the idyllic garden party turned into a vision of Man in the throes of systematic collapse. With little or no cover grey faces peered from under bushes, soggy tuna paste sandwiches were consumed next to giant overflowing bins, summer dresses clung to bodies like cellophane, bedraggled children sobbed uncontrollably and apprehensive-looking[15] men slipped whilst carrying giant trays of refreshments on the lawns of the picnic area, Aorangi Park[vii], covering cream trousers with thick mud.

The only positive aspect of the deluge seemed to be the fact that everyone suddenly started talking to each other, as if remembering that they all had a lot in common, just by actually being there, being soaking wet and waiting aimlessly around.

As the rain became heavier it became apparent, like some kind of existential play, that we were now queuing for nothing. We were waiting for our own Godot, and he was nowhere to be seen. On we queued, my Mum was not one for giving up, having been known to admonish me for trying to get a day off school when claiming illness with the harsh, but

---

14 Lightning is pretty terrifying, and is responsible for about 4,000 deaths a year. More encouragingly, out of every ten people hit, nine will survive. For comparison's sake an average of eight people are killed by sharks each year and 12 while taking a selfie.

15 Drunk, I now realise.

admittedly effective, line of, 'What would Jimmy Connors do? Would he give up or would he go to school?' Looking back it was slightly surreal, the idea of a 34-year-old multi-millionaire tennis player attending my primary school, but it did the job with me.

By 6pm it became clear that there would be no change in the weather as a kind of World War II megaphone system pumped out the information I had been dreading; there would be no further play at the All England Championships that day.

'Ladies and gentlemen, can I have your attention please. We are expecting this rain to continue. In view of this, the referee has decided there will be no further play tonight.'

It would become a common refrain over the years.

A NATION OF SHOPKEEPERS

The Wimbledon Shop[16] seemed to exist primarily to sell player postcards, which I collected avidly. In fact, I collected everything at that age; rubbers, marbles, football stickers, old tobacco boxes, dead insects. It's a wonder I didn't become a serial killer. Postcards of people with thrillingly exotic names like Manuela Maleeva, Wally Masur, Christo Van Rensburg, Carling Bassett, Gigi Fernandez and, my personal favourite aged ten, the American, Peanut Louie. I bought everything I could afford – at 5p each that was about 12 cards, with players from behind the 'Iron Curtain' seeming incredibly exotic and collectible, particularly as I thought it actually was a curtain, running from Poland down to Romania and made of a kind of chain mail.

SMELLS LIKE TEEN SPIRIT

From reading the sports section of my Dad's *Daily Telegraph* I had also started to piece together bits of information about my new German favourite, Boris Becker, who was still very much six years older than me, now at the ripe old age of 17. In early June I had seen the articles about him at the Queen's Club grass court event in west London, where Johan Kriek, after losing to him, had said, 'If he plays like this, he'll win Wimbledon.' A sulky McEnroe had lost in SW19 to big-serving South African Kevin Curren, while Boris was battling on, winning lengthy matches against Henri Leconte and Anders Jarryd and finally reaching the big stage; the mythical Gentlemen's Singles Final.

Sunday, 7 July was the first day I can remember really anticipating a sporting event, getting up early and reading the paper like a grown-up, then preparing my living room

---

16 As at all the Majors this is now a multi-million pound sporting Aladdin's Den selling things like leather passport holders, branded oven gloves and Ralph Lauren babygrows. As well as really funny books about The Queue.

viewing station. Boris never looked like blowing his chance and that day he became the youngest, and first unseeded, Wimbledon champion. The so-called 'Superboy' dived and rolled all over the court like a lad possessed, in spite of having lost an incredibly taxing eight sets on the way to achieving it, playing an exhausting 292 games along the way. At the age of 11 a 17-year-old already seemed like a massive grown-up, but looking back the achievement becomes more astonishing with each passing year.

'It was a romantic tale more improbable than any fairy story. The sheer youthful joy of the lad, his disarming honesty and amazing maturity at press conferences were like a breath of fresh air after the questionable behaviour of recent years. This surely was the finest thing to have happened to Wimbledon and to tennis generally since the war.'

From John Barrett's quasi-biblical tome,
Wimbledon: The Official History

Ladies' Champion *Martina Navratilova*
Gentlemen's Champion *Boris Becker*

IF YOU CAN'T STAND THE HEAT

This was the year that the breathtaking new yellow Slazenger balls were used for the first time, largely as the white balls got stained green on the grass, sometimes making them impossible to see on TV, where tennis was being featured more and more often. It was also the year that, aged 12, I visited Wimbledon 'sans Mum' for the first time. A school pal and I headed up on the bus on the first Tuesday, quickly discovering the 'standing room' area on Centre Court, where 2,000 people could squash onto a stepped terrace, a genteel take on football's rowdier equivalent.

The section cut a swathe through the middle of Centre Court's eastern stand, boasting a louder and more raucous (it's relative) atmosphere than those in the equivalent of the stalls or the dress circle. Here you could have your own (tiny) space, if you were willing to get there early or, as you might imagine, queue for ages[viii], waiting for someone else to either:

    a) get bored

    b) need the toilet

    or c) faint.

The great benefit of being 12, dressed in school uniform, and looking like I was about seven, was that I could wriggle in to the smaller spots without too much resistance from grown-ups. On the downside there was the toilet situation. If you had enjoyed three Mr Freeze ice pops, a litre of 29p cream soda and two cans of Shandy Bass on the bus there was every chance you would, once the adrenalin of getting in to Centre Court wore off, need a jimmy riddle, normally kicking in after about five minutes. I learned the art of extreme bladder control on those unforgiving steps.

A BRIT OF ALRIGHT?

Once again my British brethren were leaving us with nothing to get behind; the only interest seemed to be around a new guy called Andrew Castle, busy challenging John Lloyd for the not-at-all coveted domestic No.1 spot[17]. Lloyd lost to South African Christo Steyn in the first round, bringing his retirement forward as a result. 'LLOYD QUITS IN TEARS' and 'HORROR SHOW IS FINAL CURTAIN', *The Sun* sympathetically reviewed. Castle actually went two sets to one up against second seed, Mats Wilander, in the second round, but eventually lost in five.

I'll BE BACK

I had recently become obsessed by the film *Rocky IV,* in which an ageing, grey marl-clad Sylvester Stallone took on the full power of the Soviet might, in the form of the cyborg-esque Ivan Drago. He did this with the help of some serious soft-rock guitar riffs and a lot of log-pulling in the snow, ultimately achieving his goal of single-handedly solving the Cold War. I was therefore pleased that we had our very own

---

17 Castle would go on to reach number 80 in the world and carve himself out a wildly successful career at just 'Being Andrew Castle' on television.

Drago in the form of Ivan Lendl, the cartoon villain of world tennis whose first *Sports Illustrated* cover was accompanied by the rather spiteful headline, 'The Champion No-one Cares About'. At this point the man who would partly transform my tennis life (26 years later) was a cartoon caricature to me, the nemesis to my faves – from the flamboyant McEnroe, the people's champion Jimbo and the hyperactive schoolboy, Boris. Lendl's sombre wit and caustic humour were hidden behind that iron curtain and playground stories circulated about how he only ate raw fish and chicken livers, trained for 18 hours a day in a desert on his exact replica of the Centre Court (relaid blade-by-blade) and slept in a cryogenically freezing space tent, like Michael Jackson.

LOVE, HONOUR & OBEY

The Honorary Stewards at the All England Club were fascinating to watch. They all wore cream chinos with navy blue blazers and generally acted like the kind of people you would like to bump in to if you were looking for an ice cream stall, your best friend had got locked in the bog or you'd

lost your shoes. Many of the HSs had those walking sticks that really posh people have with a kind of leather and steel seat which folds out, allowing them to sit down anywhere. They are all terribly, and genuinely, interested in your story as to how you found yourself numbered 14,546th in The Queue that day, trained in some kind of secret academy deep underground where raised voices are silenced with a glance and even the most unsavoury of incidents (pushing in, normally) is dealt with using the upmost discretion[ix]. I wondered why they didn't replace the normal police with these folk, they seemed to be making such a good job of it all.

ROBO-BOBO

In the 1980s all tennis players seemed glamorous and three-dimensional, with personalities so colourful that they felt like movie stars. Brooding Slobodan Zivojinovic was a case in point. 'Bobo' came from the Eastern Bloc, was over 15 feet tall and had a serve like a missile launcher. Years later his announcement that he had had an intimate friendship with Princess Di cemented his place in the most outlandish of tennis's X-Files;

'In our first conversation she asked me if I am the tennis player with the fastest serve and I said, "Yes". Then she asked if my serve was still good. Shortly after that we started seeing each other.'

It was that simple in the 80s. Allegedly[x].

POSSESSION IS NINE-TENTHS OF THE LAW

1986 was a Wimbledon which lacked McEnroe, who had decided, like a crabby teenager still missing his mate Björn, to 'take a year off'[18]. It was also a significant year for my

---

18 A decision he may well have lived to regret, seeing as he would never again reach a Major final, and only three more semi-finals.

German hero Boris Becker, as he continued his rise up the world rankings, attracting the most attention coming in to the tournament as the defending champion. This superstar status was accentuated by the fact that he had a bloke in his camp who was tennis's equivalent to Colonel Tom Parker. Ion Tiriac was also referred to as a 'manager' but unlike Tom he came from Transylvania and was presumably not shaving off 50 per cent of Boris's earnings and about to launch him into a career of rubbish films with names like *Girls! Girls! Girls!*, *Clambake* and *Tickle Me*.

Some kids at school had mocked my Teutonic fandom, citing the relatively recent incidents of two large world wars, and our general dislike in a sporting sense for all things German, ergo, successful. But I was there, with my friend Jonathan, to watch BB in two of the matches on the way, as we employed pleading facial expressions and a lot of neck craning to get right to the front and see him pound down some heavy artillery.

In the semis Boris saw off Henri Leconte, a match I remember more for the fact that Leconte looked happier in defeat than Becker did in victory[xi], a particular trait of the French male tennis player in the modern era. By the final I had started to take things for granted. I just assumed Boris would win, because that is what I wanted to happen.

Ivan Lendl was obsessed by winning Wimbledon, which Boris knew, allowing him to play carefree tennis, with absolute abandon. Ion Tiriac watched impassively from the box, chain-smoking and looking like he was pulling strings on a much bigger scale somewhere in Eastern Europe. Or possibly lining up a film deal. After Becker's straight sets win he said of Centre Court: 'It feels like it is my court.' What could possibly go wrong?

Ladies' Champion *Martina Navratilova*
Gentlemen's Champion *Boris Becker*

DON'T MENTION THE WAR

'The Great Storm', an extratropical cyclone, battered southern England early in '87. It was a tragic event but also well-known for the fact that weatherman Michael Fish actually said that night on national television, 'Earlier on today, apparently, a woman rang the BBC and said she heard there was a hurricane on the way ... well, if you're watching, don't worry, there isn't!'

I departed the storm-flattened country, travelling on an aeroplane for the first time in my life, having only previously visited 'The Continent', as everyone used to refer to France and Spain, in our silver Ford Escort Mk2. BB was now, particularly in McEnroe's continued absence, my firm favourite, and in March I boarded the Lufthansa flight parent-less, bound for Germany to see his homeland. I was staying with a dysfunctional family in their *haus* near Hanover, as the elder daughter had been an exchange student with us in London. She was great, but had literally run away from home by the time I got there, leaving her German kid brother,

~~Adolf~~ Dieter, who was as fat as a pudding and obsessed with his toy soldiers and the Second World War. I imagine he has probably been put in some kind of secure institution by now, but back then he liked to play slightly unsettling war games or 'show & tell' sessions, in which he would proudly display his hunting knife collection and tell me how 'best' to cut through someone's windpipe from behind. As an unstable 13-year-old with a seemingly complete absence of friends, this hobby struck me as a bad idea even then.

As the trip was all about Boris I was delighted by the fact that he was on TV almost constantly and on the cover of pretty much every magazine I could find around the house. I had only been learning German at school for about four months, so I could order Black Forest gateau and reserve hotel rooms for a family of four, but needed some help from the family when BB was interviewed on a game show. I was most excited by the visit to a local Intersport shop in their BMW 7-Series, which even had cut-outs of *Mein Herö* in the car park. Dieter stayed in the car. He was angry about something, Poland maybe. The visit meant I could get all the new BB PUMA kit my savings would allow; trainers, shorts, socks, t-shirt and racket bag – the polo was just beyond my paper-round finances. A week later I wore it all down to the newsagents in south London, even carrying the bag, and walked home gingerly as I was being circled by kids from the estate calling me names I won't repeat.

BORIS GETS PHILOSOPHICAL (ME, HYSTERICAL)

Having shocked the world by retaining his Wimbledon crown in 1986 I was sure that a historic treble would put Boris on the road to besting the incredible five straight wins achieved by his alliterative predecessor Björn Borg[xii] from 1976–80. A comfortable first round was followed on the Friday (rain had delayed the start of the week) by the fairly straightforward job of despatching Peter Doohan, a respected Aussie pro, but very beatable for someone like Becker. In fact, he had beaten Doohan very comfortably at Queen's two weeks previously, on his way to winning the event again. Doohan was one of the old-school Antipodeans who played with style, fought like dogs, won or lost like men and then had a beer with you afterwards.[xiii]

What followed that afternoon would scar me for years, shatter my fragile belief system, and teach me some important life lessons.

'I didn't lose a war. Nobody died. I just lost a tennis match. I tried as hard as I could, I didn't play well. He played very well.'

This was Boris's famously philosophical post-match statement, but to me it was way more important than war or death. I couldn't compute it, I was gobsmacked, I was flabbergasted. I'd already experienced two moments of the very worst football miserableness – the World Cup in '82 in Spain when England went out without losing and then in Mexico '86 when cheating Diego robbed us and Gary Lineker missed an open goal. But this was tennis, it was more personal, and Boris had just gone down in four sets to a man the papers were calling 'impoverished'. The 'Boy Kaiser' had been 'bonked out of Wimbledon'. 'DOOHAN AND OUT!', 'THE BECKER WRECKER!' and 'HE COULDN'T GIVE A XXXX'[xiv], the headlines screamed. Becker showed admirable class in never once blaming himself but bowing at the feet of the world No.70, going on to say, 'I'm not immortal … it

was like playing a man with a magic wand.' Amazingly not one newspaper used this quote with the headline, 'WIZARD OF OZ'.

BLAST FROM THE PAST

On the Saturday, suffering from an acute teen depression, I dragged a friend along to queue, in an attempt to try and banish my demons. I managed to get on to No.2 Court to see Pat Cash step in to the breach with a chessboard headband, a highlighted mullet and a bit of diving around. For me it was Boris-Lite, but it was still better than nothing.

On the Tuesday the 76-year-old American, Jimmy Connors, staged one of the greatest comebacks in tennis history on a rowdy No.1 Court in the fourth round. Facing young gunslinger, world No.20 Mikael Pernfors, Connors played like a drain in front of an almost silent crowd, watching in disbelief. The great battler, the Basher of Belleville, the self-styled 'Rough Diamond', quietly went down 1-6, 1-6, 1-4, as history finally caught up with his ageing legs. He was as dead as disco, as I'd heard an American behind me say.

And then, quite incredibly, like a rusty old ship turning slowly in a deep sea harbour, Jimbo began to turn it around, clawing his way back in to the third set and going on to actually win 1-6, 1-6, 7-5, 6-4, 6-2. Asked afterwards what happened he replied, in trademark matter-of-fact delivery, 'My ego was hurt ... so I had to do something about it.' For some reason I have always imagined a Vegas-era Elvis delivering this line.

THE SPORTING PLAYGROUND

The 1987 Ladies' Finals Day saw Martina win an incredible sixth title on the bounce, seeing off her old pal Chris Evert in the semis and new kid on the block, Steffi Graf, in the final[xv]. Cash overcame an exhausted Jimbo in the semi-finals before going on to lift the trophy on the Sunday, dishing out another straight sets defeat for Lendl in the final, barely able to disguise a covetous gaze at the trophy. Cash then broke protocol, and almost his legs, by climbing all over the Centre Court walls, on his way up to his coaches and family in the box[xvi]. The hapless Ivan must have really fancied his chances in the final this year, what with Boris out of the way, and McEnroe totally out of it somewhere else. Surely his time would come? 439 miles away in Glasgow, someone called Andrew Barron Murray had just been born.

Ladies' Champion *Martina Navratilova*
Gentlemen's Champion *Pat Cash*

KEEP OFF THE GRASS

During the winter I would get my Wimbledon fix by hopping on the 164 bus and heading up to the All England Club Museum on an almost monthly basis. I loved gazing at the old kit, trophies and thousands of photos of William Renshaw, Lottie Dodd, Spencer Gore and my favourite old-timer, Fred Perry. Three of us from school went along in February. One was my new-found tennis friend, Bally, pronounced 'Ball-ee'. Bally was not his real name, but it was the nickname he had been awarded at my school, based on the fact that he owned 'over 500' used tennis balls, due to having a garden which backed on to Sutton Churches Tennis Club, whose members were clearly a little wayward with their forehands. Another lad who tagged along, called Spencer Dartington, was so snooty, and out of place at my state grammar school, that he was once almost lynched when he turned up to Mufti Day in a green wax cloak and polka dot neckerchief.

A museum ticket also allowed you to stand on the Centre Court 'viewing balcony' and gaze at the whole arena in its real, living, breathing glory. In the absence of security on the balcony that day we took our chance and hopped over the wall to explore the rest of the empty grounds. Knowing the layout of the All England like a WW2 spy landing in enemy territory I was able to guide us swiftly through to the hallowed entrance of my favourite, No.1 Court, then situated just next door.

We walked out blinking into the sunlight and stood in the middle of the court, like we had landed on the moon. It was easily the most exciting thing to happen to me since Live Aid. Bemused and overawed, we decided to put on the headbands we had just bought from the Club shop and start a game of 'imagination tennis', much like real tennis but with no lines, balls, rackets or net. It was great fun until a giant warning siren pierced the arena and four burly security guards ran on to the court from all sides. I was the one who got my collar felt as the other two headbands disappeared into the stands. Fifteen minutes later we all found ourselves standing in an office somewhere underground as the angry elders phoned each of our parents to tell them in detail about our crimes and the inevitable punishment to follow. I was just worried that the criminal record I was about to receive would prevent me from entering my beloved Gate 4 in exactly 127 days, and counting. My worst fears were allayed with a cuff round the back of the neck from the guard. In those days an adult could whack any child who stepped out of line and I had been clouted loads of times by strangers, all over south London. I should really get therapy. On the plus side I had managed to steal a piece of grass from the corner, which I planted at the back of our garden.

HERO, ZERO, BIGGER HERO

This was the year I extended my queuing to another London borough, W14, for the Wimbledon tune-up event at Queen's Club, providing one of the more eventful days of my young life. Hanging around outside the players' entrance in the hope of seeing some big names, you can imagine my delight when Bally and I watched Boris himself come striding through the doors, carrying about 20 rackets and almost glowing with his huge physical presence. We were the only people there so I went forward first, nervously asking Boris to sign my programme. He walked straight past, completely blanking me. Bally, aggrieved on my behalf, had another go, only to be met with a very peremptory 'No', and an aggressive hand block, like a trademark stop volley. I was totally crestfallen. We watched my hero walk away, along the path by the side of a hedge, with no one else around. Bally summed it up perfectly: 'What a git.'

And then it happened. Staring at the empty passage Boris had vacated, I saw the greatest sight of my life, as he reappeared in the distance and beckoned us over. Yes, us. We legged it up the path towards the big man who actually apologised for being rude – there was no one else around, why did he care what two snotty-nosed kids thought? – before sitting on the bonnet of his Mercedes 500 SEC and starting to chat. I asked him how he was feeling for Wimbledon, about the guy he was playing that day and he talked freely like we were old pals. He then found his own page in our programmes, signed personal messages to us both, shook our hands and casually high-fived us like old buddies. It was like being touched by God.[19]

STREET DREAMS ARE MADE OF THIS

I took my queuing etiquette up another sizeable level in 1988 when taking the thrilling step of sleeping out overnight for the first time. The nocturnal Queue system was then far from the organised event you find now in Wimbledon

---

19 The same thing sort of happened to me with Virginia Wade in 1990 at Wimbledon, but that time she didn't reappear from behind the hedge, we didn't speak further and she didn't act at all like we were old pals.

Park, as you simply took a crash barrier from the verge like a vagrant and built yourself a small pen on the pavement. You then created your home for the night using materials you had brought along. For The Queue-hardened this involved inflatable double beds, tables and chairs, barbecues, portable televisions, lighting with small generators, hairdryers, slippers and dressing gowns. Giant clamps would be used to fit the square space out with a tarpaulin, net doorways would be hung and cardboard boxes laid on the floor for the final touch. I was pretty sure some had a 'There's No Place Like Home' framed cross-stitch hanging on the side barrier as you entered.

For Bally and I the process involved two sleeping bags, 50 discarded copies of the *Daily Mail* as mattresses and dustbin liners by way of waterproofing. As I attempted to fasten my bin bags to the fence using elastic bands a bloke walking past laughed out loud and shouted, 'You'd have better luck nailing a jelly to a wall.' I was cross, but it seemed a reasonable observation. It rained off and on throughout that first night, this lack of proper impervious kit costing us dear, as the *Daily Mail*s started to moisten and then mould around our legs.

I should point out that on the given night, Friday, 24 June, my Mum and her South London Queue Association[20] were also in attendance, a fact I tried to ignore as Bally and I set ourselves up just one hundred metres down the pavement. We tried to pretend we were doing it on our own, but did need leftovers from their well-planned, if slightly vinous, picnic.

RAINY NIGHT WITH PEOPLE FROM GEORGIA

We made our first Queue friends that night, a couple from Atlanta, Georgia who were the biggest people I had ever seen and introduced themselves to us in that brilliantly

---

20 Don't ask. They had badges. I 'designed' them.

direct American way, 'Hi, I'm Troy, and this is my good wife, Monique.' It was totally un-British and as a result we totally loved it. The transatlantic love-in was cemented when they started to share sweets with us. Aged 14 I considered myself a kind of confectionery sommelier, but these new American vintages blew my tiny mind. For the record Reese's peanut butter pieces are sensational, Milk Duds are the thinking teen's Malteser and Hershey Kisses taste like dog treats.

GIFTS THAT KEEP ON GIVING

One of the most exciting moments of the day came shortly after dawn when the first newspaper sellers would arrive, bringing with them the much-desired order of play. Before the internet existed the papers were a feast for weary eyes, and at Wimbledon they came with an added bonus in the form of free gifts. That day the *Daily Express* gave away a tennis-themed bum bag, the *Daily Telegraph* a visor and the *Daily Mail* one of those money holders you could take in the sea, should you feel the need to swim with a tube of pound coins wrapped around your neck. The now-defunct *TODAY*, the nation's first colour newspaper, weighed in with a towel! Huge ink costs plus this kind of profligate merchandising plan may be part of the reason that paper no longer exists.

REBEL WITHOUT A PLACE IN THE THIRD ROUND

I had started to really hone my McEnroe appreciation, in almost perfect synergy with the waning of his other-worldly powers. Looking increasingly like a man with a fork in a world of soup[xvii], his return to Wimbledon after a two-year sabbatical had been disastrous to say the least, and I was there in the bowels of Centre Court standing room to see him unravel further. It came against the strong, if unspectacular,

71

Australian, Wally Masur, in only the second round, back when tennis players thought nothing of having names like 'Wally'.

McEnroe was all temper and no talent that day, at one point going doolally at an odd Scottish lady who appeared to be his biggest fan. After every error she would plead out loud, 'Oh come orrrrnnn, John', as if she was asking him to put the rubbish out before coming to bed. It wasn't helped by the fact that she was wearing a homemade sweatshirt emblazoned with the felt letters:

JOHN McENROE

steam-ironed on to the material at a lopsided angle. He lost in straight sets and I wondered if he would ever bother coming back. 'BRAT BEATEN BY A WALLY', said one of the tabloids[xviii], and it was hard to disagree. It had to be acknowledged that McEnroe on an off-day could be really, thoroughly, foul, both to opponents and fans, and it was never pleasant or easy to watch him torture himself and others. There was absolutely no levity or lightness to be found in him, or the experience of watching him.

CUTS BOTH WAYS

During his emotionally-draining semi-final win against Lendl, Boris gave the world an insight into his brilliantly loopy private head space for the first time. With his thick strawberry (how fitting) blond hair now long and untamed, he looked like a cross between Diana Spencer in 1980 and 'Do Ya Think I'm Sexy?' era Rod Stewart. He grew so irritated by these locks that at one point he took matters into his own hands during a changeover and started hacking at his fringe with some nail scissors. 'HAIRY FOR BORIS' and 'HERR KUTT', the papers[xix] guffawed.

MONDAY, MONDAY

The rain had been falling all week and the Sunday was almost a complete washout, meaning the majority of the Gentlemen's Final was played on the Monday. It would be the first in a three-year final trilogy between Becker and likeable Swede Stefan Edberg[21], who looked a bit like a model from a C&A catalogue and had the oddest forehand action in the world. Edberg won that day[22], and became the first person ever to beat Boris Becker on his beloved Centre Court. I thought it was just nice to see the big manchild get beyond the second round and go easy on the award-winning speeches. His *schwester* Steffi Graf won her first Ladies' title before going on to win something truly unique that year; the Golden Slam, which was all four Majors, plus the Olympic gold medal.

---

21 Edberg first came to the world's attention in tragic circumstances when he was playing in the Boys' event at the US Open in 1983. He served an emphatic ace which hit the line judge, Dick Wertheim, in the groin, sending him crashing to the hard ground with force and causing severe head injuries. He passed away five days later and, whilst not actually killed by the impact of the serve, Edberg was understandably deeply affected by it all.

22 In 1988, all the Gentlemen's Majors were won by Swedes with Mats Wilander, possibly the most underrated player of all time and barely a footnote in Wimbledon history, incredibly winning all of the other three. It's a shame, as he was one of the most engaging of all the men in the modern era.

Ladies' Champion *Steffi Graf*
Gentlemen's Champion *Stefan Edberg*

THE BECKER WRECKER ON THE DISTRICT LINE

After a day at Queen's in June, I boarded the tube train at Baron's Court and could barely believe my eyes when none other than 'THE BECKER WRECKER' walked on with bags of gear and rackets and sat right opposite me. No one else on the tube would have had a clue who he was, but I was not going to let this pass. I politely enquired, and had it confirmed, that he was indeed Peter Doohan and, despite the fact that I needed to get off at Earl's Court, I stayed on and chatted to (or 'at') him until we reached Victoria. I started out calling him 'Mr Doohan', for some reason, but you can't stop once you start, it's tricky to suddenly go informal, like the 'vous–tu' switch in French. It didn't seem to matter, as Mr Doohan was incredibly friendly, especially as he was being interrogated by a 15-year-old with a freakishly exhaustive knowledge of his life.

MAC THE KNIFE ... EDGE

On the first Tuesday, the art of getting a decent spot in standing room on Centre Court now down pat (full school uniform, lots of wide-eyed smiling), we had prime places for the Return of the Mac. He had sort of returned in '88 but that was just a teething problem, right? Darren 'Killer' Cahill, the up-and-coming Australian he would face in the first round, looked a worryingly bad draw, particularly as the now 30-year-old McEnroe had not played a competitive singles match for two months. After his 86/87 hiatus this was a man on the brink; out of step, out of fashion and clearly out of his mind to be trying to scale the lofty heights of yesteryear, they said.

A packed Centre Court watched in resignation as McEnroe dug himself into a two-set hole, looking like a relic of a past era. I was peering out from the edges of the enclosed standing area, desperate to spend a penny for the last two hours but unable to bear losing my place for fear of not getting back in. It was as if my bladder was controlling his destiny; as long as I didn't pee McEnroe was still in Wimbledon.

I watched in horror (and increasing pain) as one of my irascible heroes played like a zero and my belief system started to crumble around me. He looked angry, frustrated, confused and jittery, hitting an almost laughable 18 double faults that day, the equivalent to handing your opponent four and a half games for free.

And then, for no apparent reason, everything changed. A wily McEnroe went toe-to-toe with Cahill, first showing grit and then genius as he suddenly started to look like he was enjoying the fight. He had never previously been known for this, he was van Gogh, the artist's artist, and battling victories from the jaws of defeat were what a blunt instrument like Connors did. If McEnroe was off-colour, so be it, he didn't tend to grit it out. Lobs, those huge wound-up swinging serves, touch volleys, arrowed and ripped backhand winners from seemingly impossible angles, they all flowed like '84, as the bemused crowd swung overwhelmingly to his side and swept him to an emotional five-set victory. I had almost developed a bacterial infection of the urinary tract, but at least Mac was in the second round.

DARK ARTS OF THE TEENAGE TICKET TOUT

Still not being able to go to the toilet without feeling pain, I decided that the standing room situation needed to be addressed. While the charity boxes held all the returns, you could position yourself to intercept the departing people by asking if they had finished with their tickets – so effectively swindling the charity out of cash, morals not being my strong point at this stage. The magical gangway between Centre and No.1 Court was like Shark Alley for a bloodthirsty teenage ticket hustler, as you could effortlessly get returned tickets from rich, carefree strangers with nothing more than an angelic smile, giving you full access to a vast number of seats, according to where the best action was. With Brits largely absent from any thrills that year it was all about the big names; Lendl down a set on No.1? Head for your fifth row courtside spot, or get a bigger perspective from up in the gods. McEnroe getting twitchy holding serve? Back on Centre, Block 101, next to the Royal Box.

By Thursday, my ticket racket in full effect, I held over 30 showcourt seats, like a young Artful Dodger, skilled and cunning, but with no Fagin controlling me. I would occasionally dish them out to the Wimbledon High School girls, enjoying my role as 'the kid with the stash', lurking in my favoured position outside Block 302 in the bowels of Centre Court. On the second Monday I counted up the tickets and I had over 70, plus all the ones I had given away to the pretty girls. Realistically, I had almost 100 in total, with a street value of over £4,000. I think my parents were getting quizzical as I started spending more time in my room, counting and recounting my collection (of essentially worthless pieces of paper) which I then stuck on to a giant piece of paper and Blu Tac'd to my bedroom door so I could stare at it from my bed.

CHRISSIE

Looking back, it seemed that modern tennis's boom period, or modern 'Golden Age', started to draw in around about now. This era was embodied by the tennis world's favourite girl-next-door, Chris Evert, who bowed out this year, still seeded No.4, but blown away by the all-conquering Steffi Graf in the semi-finals. She departed with class, turning to the crowd with an almost regal smile and wave, her place in the pantheon of greats as secure as anyone's.

Evert would retire at the end of the year with an impressive 18 Majors[23] and with the most incredible record of having reached the semi-finals in 273 of the 303 tournaments she entered. Loved for her ladylike demeanour and pursed lips in the face of adversity, 'Chrissie', as she was affectionately known, was actually a competitor every bit as gritty as her great adversary, and friend, Martina. Their rivalry stands alone in the sport (maybe in any sport) for both its ferocity and its longevity but mostly for the incredible warmth they displayed towards each other throughout, in spite of their wildly contrasting personalities and styles. It's easy to be all cosy and nostalgic when you look back on a highlights reel in a TV studio 20 years later but these two were proper chums

---

23 The same number as Martina finished up with.

from the off and could show each other genuine affection at the net after duking it out on court for three hours in a heatwave. Their battles ran from 1973 to 1989 and even lasted a period in the middle when Martina beat her friend 14 times on the trot[24]. Evert, showing that grit which ran through her, came back from the losing run to wrestle more wins, but she also knew her time had come to go and she was never the type to outstay her welcome.

THIRD TIME'S THE CHARM

Steffi once again frustrated Martina in the final, as her quest to claim a record ninth title continued to prove elusive. I pointedly remember the commentators' insistence on referring to her partner, a lady called Judy Nelson, as her 'friend', every time they panned over the players' box. Even at 15 I was pretty sure the rest of the adult world could deal with the fact that Martina was gay, emphasising how uncool sport still was around the subject of homosexuality[25].

After the trauma of '87 and the relative acceptance of '88 I was also delighted to see my hero back where he belonged, dancing the night away with Steffi at the Champions' Ball, as a second final with Edberg had brought a third title for Boris, and the world was back in order.

---

24 Not to be confused with Vitas Gerulaitis's famed 16-match losing streak to Jimmy Connors which he broke at the 17th attempt before giving a press conference in which, before being asked a question, he emphatically opened with, 'And let that be a lesson to you all. Nobody ... but nobody ... beats Vitas Gerulaitis 17 times in a row.'

25 Even lovable sports commentator, the late Harry Carpenter, once said of 60s star, Maria Bueno, 'I was utterly appalled when I found out the Brazilian star was a lesbian. I couldn't help thinking it was such a waste. She had stunning natural black hair and a beautiful face with a flawless complexion.' As reported in the *Daily Mail*.

Damen-Champion *Steffi Graf*
Herren-Champion *Boris Becker*

HOW *NOT* TO DRESS FOR WIMBLEDON

PART 1: GENTS

Fashion flamboyance for men is a no-no and you should never indulge the desire to try too hard. Remember the old maxim: 'Women in fashion, men in classics.'

1. Straw hats are effective, but can also look like a massive affectation. If you must, go simple and classic, remembering that the fedora was only just carried off by Jackson in '84, and that was an era when he could get away with wearing just one glove, covered in plastic rhinestones.

2. Wearing sunglasses on top of your head is acceptable for functional, but not sartorial, use – i.e. you've just stepped out of the sun and your hands are full.

3. Little trainer socks are not a high point in men's fashion history, but if you do suffer from sweaty feet then make sure they are in no way visible above the shoe.

4. Chinos should be vibrant and not those awful muddy sand-coloured ones they sell in Sunday supplements for £19.99, or two pairs for £24.99.

5. No jeans. Ever.

6. Union Jacks, obviously, in any form.

7. Don't dress like you are actually going to play tennis. This is the same as wearing football boots to go and watch a match at Wembley, as if you are hoping to get a game.

8. Cable-knit rowing sweaters tied around the shoulders can only be carried off by those Italians who dress like they are going to a *Brideshead Revisited* party.

9. Brightly coloured trainers are for teenage girls and children.

10. As an overall rule, don't dress like a child, and also don't dress your child like a little grown-up in a button-down Ralphy and chinos. It's just weird.

11. The only thing worse than sandals are 'designer sandals' and both should be reserved for going to fancy dress parties as one of the disciples.

12. Vests are sometimes considered 't-shirts for a hot summer's day' but they are in fact underwear and only consider if you also think that y-fronts are 'little trousers for a hot summer's day'.

13. If you are wondering about flip flops then you should not even be reading this, stop immediately.

THE BIG SLEEP

1990 was the year of my final GCSE exams, meaning a favourable timetable would see me done and dusted by early June, giving me a proper tilt at The Queue. The plan Bally and I hatched was an audacious one – we were going for the maximum attendance, 11 straight nights on the streets, from the first Sunday to the second Wednesday, the whole period showcourt tickets were available to buy on the day. Like two young mountaineers going from climbing the stairs in year one to attempting Everest in year two[26], we were going all-out, requiring a fully briefed and prep'd support team (parents) plus some serious financial backing (money saved from paper rounds and gardening work). While some of my friends were planning a trip to Glastonbury to see The Happy Mondays play in a field I was gearing up for the bigger thrills of 'The First Monday' on the immaculate lawns of SW19.

We arrived in the new unified queue location on Church Road at 8am on Sunday, 24 June, placed 25th and 26th respectively, and armed with a solid amount of food, considering we were two people. I personally contributed:

---

26 In actual fact over 500 people climb Everest every year.

By 8am on Monday I had two oranges and half a cucumber left.

THE DAILY GRIND

After an excellent first day in scorching sun we were back in The Queue and now friends with some slightly loopy alcoholics from Bournemouth. We established a solid relationship in which they were perma-sozzled and saw us as perma-hungry, needing to be perma-fed, as if our feeding times had been taken on as their responsibility in some way.

A standard day over the next week or so went something like this:

> *8pm – Leave the grounds after a day of tennis, very hungry, and head for the left luggage office by Gate 5. Pick up tarpaulin, camp bed and sleeping bag.*
>
> *8.10pm – Join Queue in Church Road, average position: around the early 80-somethings.*
>
> *8.15pm – Start to set up base camp, starting with crash barrier walls.*
>
> *8.17pm – Finalise base camp set up with tarpaulin ceiling.*
>
> *8.18pm – Discuss our levels of hunger and count coins. Hope a parent might be bringing a takeaway.*
>
> *8.30pm – Walk to fish & chip or burger van, buy as many chips as possible and steal minimum of ten sachets of mayonnaise, brown sauce and tomato ketchup.*
>
> *8.45pm – Talk nonsense (3+ hours).*
>
> *1.00am – Sleep.*
>
> *2.00am – Be awoken by cars driving past, sounding horns as 'a laugh'.*
>
> *3.00am – Be awoken by cars driving past, sounding horns as 'a laugh'.*
>
> *3.30am – Be awoken by cars driving past, sounding … oh, you get it.*

6.00am – Awoken by steward. Very hungry.

6.30am – Reawoken by steward, more sternly.

7.00am – Walk to toilet hut, smell bacon cooking nearby, ingest odour, return to base camp. Eat sachets of sauce. Hope the alcoholics might be too hungover to eat their breakfast.

7.15am – Pack up base camp, buy newspaper, sit on floor. Eat last sachet of sauce.

9.15am – Move forward two metres. Hope the alcoholics have started drinking, thus losing all interest in food.

10.00am – Buy tickets and enter grounds. Leave tarpaulin, camp bed and sleeping bag in left luggage office.

11.00am – Play begins on outside courts. Hungry. Talk a lot about food. Maybe watch some people eating food at one of the many stalls.

2.00pm – Play begins on showcourts [27]. Extreme hunger kicks in.

MEAT TO LIVE

On Tuesday we were invited to our first ever social function at the All England Club. I say 'invited', it was more of a 'mention'. Queue regulars, Derek and Cynthia, part of the group of heavy-drinking and slightly bonkers Dorsets, had kindly sent word that they would be hosting a barbecue at their crash barrier home from 8pm, in order to screen the England v Belgium World Cup second round match on their four-inch TV screen. We sent word that we would be delighted to attend.

Barbecued burgers and sausages were washed down with warm cans of Sainsbury's lager, all of which we greeted as if we were discovering the concept of food and drink for the first

---

27 This seemed very late, but was apparently linked to the 1900s when it would take the Royals that long to get across town from the Palace. They should have used the District Line.

time. As we were in the early stages of severe calorific energy deficiency, one of the energies which is needed to maintain human life, I genuinely think I had eight burgers in the first hour, sending my body into a kind of meat and sugar spasm. Fortunately they were the kind of people who saw the wolfing down of eight burgers as a compliment to the chef, rather than the behaviour of a greedy hog. The night turned into a right old knees-up and when David Platt hooked in a last-minute winner we all danced in the streets (me, maniacally, I was coming up on the burgers), marking one of only two occasions in my life[28] when international football would actually out-charm tennis in terms of success and overall enjoyment.

KNEE DEEP

The next morning, possibly due to the squiffy effect of the Sainsbury's lager consumed and the spasming, I did something very stupid. Whilst leaning against the crash barrier as we waited to go into the grounds, and overly attentive to the university-age girls turning up for work in their pretty

28 The other to come in 1996.

dresses, I pushed my knee too far between the steel bars of the structure. At first I pretended that I couldn't get free as a joke, but this rapidly degenerated into the most embarrassing situation of my life. Bally started laughing hysterically when I discreetly told him that I really could not get my leg out, as The Queue started to move and I was literally not able to join, unless I carried the eight-foot barrier with me. In no time a small group had gathered as various folk took it upon themselves to massage my knee and an Honorary Steward was dispatched to deal with the escalating situation. I felt like a motorway accident, as everyone walking past slowed down to nose/laugh.

After half an hour the unthinkable happened as a bright red fire engine pulled up and three huge firemen came over with what looked like giant joke pliers. They told me to 'Put some elbow grease in, sunshine', to which I politely replied that that was precisely what I had been doing for the best part of an hour, leaving me with a knee swollen to the size of a large coconut. Much guffawing later and the bars were slightly bent, allowing my now ridiculously inflamed joint to break free. It was humiliation on a grand scale as I was escorted back to my rightful place in The Queue, from where I hobbled to the First Aid room and then to the eighth row of Centre, opposite the umpire. From that day on The Queue People called me 'Barrier Boy'. Bally put it most succinctly, 'You're such a plank.'

GRUNTFEST

In the middle of the week the *Daily Mail* ran a strangely titled story called 'THANK HEAVENS FOR LITTLE GIRLS', which featured 14-year-old world No.13 Jennifer Capriati, and 16-year-old world No.3 Monica Seles, fresh from winning her first Major in Paris. I met Ms Seles outside the grounds on the Thursday. I am sure she remembers it as well as I do, as she giggled uncontrollably at every single thing I said, making me seem incredibly witty, or her seem like she was slightly unhinged.

Her meteoric rise was being somewhat overshadowed by her cacophonous grunting, picked up by the *Daily Mirror* and *The Sun* who both employed courtside 'Gruntometers'; one claiming that, at '91.7 decibels ... she is louder than a train and almost as loud as a pneumatic drill.' Peter Ustinov, never one to miss a tennis soundbite, chimed in with, 'I pity the neighbours on her wedding night', which sounded like the punchline to an anecdote on the Michael Parkinson show in the 1970s.

SWEETS FOR OUR SWEET

One-woman Centre Court ticket vacuum Princess Diana was in the news when she completely cracked up as a pied wagtail flew in to Centre Court during a Gentlemen's match. The newspapers couldn't take their eyes off her in the Royal Box, one reporting that she had 'scoffed a whole box of toffee',[xx] which seemed unlikely, to look at her.

LOSERS, WEEPERS

If Jeremy Bates didn't exist then Richard Curtis would have written him, with his plucky approach, 'have a go' attitude and 'just off the sailboat on the Norfolk Broads' windswept hair. Bates carried the hopes of a nation all the way to the second round, where he was stopped by McEnroe slayer, Derrick Rostagno. Andrew Castle lost in the first, along with a couple of others I had barely heard of, and it summed it all up when the biggest British stir was caused by John Lloyd saying that half the women's players were 'too fat'. He didn't specify if this was 'for tennis' or just his own personal aesthetic taste.

HISTORY IN THE MAKING

Although BB lost, in the third straight final in which he faced Stefan Edberg, I dealt with it better than I normally did a defeat for *Wünderboy*, in part as it had been such a euphoric Wimbledon all-round. On finals weekend we had, unable to tear ourselves away, headed back to the grounds for one last hurrah. Armed only with ground passes we went straight to the entrance manned by David, The Kindly Steward, where he lived up to his name by sneaking us in for the last set of the women's final. We saw Martina make history with an incredible ninth title, in her iconic white, green and purple 'MN' kit, with her pal Billie Jean watching on from her box. Having spent most of the fortnight sitting in the blazing sun, Barrier Boy had started to resemble Young Moroccan Boy. Or perhaps that was just the thick layer of dirt one acquires from sleeping rough on the streets of London for the best part of two weeks.

Ladies' Champion *Martina Navratilova*
Gentlemen's Champion *Stefan Edberg*

NEIGHBOURHOOD WATCH

Some slightly iffy A-Level mock results in January 1991 restricted me to just two nights in my beloved streetside bedroom, one of which was spent on my own next to an amorous couple from South Africa. They were initially very friendly with me and then, as we made small talk, became even more friendly with each other, to the point of my own exclusion. At one point I was telling them my fascinating, if lengthy, story of meeting Boris Becker at Queen's Club when they just started full-on snogging each other's faces off, tongues darting into each others' mouths and slobbering all over each others' necks. I didn't know what to do with myself. This was heightened about two hours later when they started enjoying a bit of slap'n'tickle in their compartment, like properly getting down to it even though we were effectively all in the same room. The Gruntometer definitely went beyond 91.7.

THE SECOND COMING

The celestial arrival of the phenomenon that was Andre Agassi was the big Wimbledon story that year. Agassi had previously been dismissed by Ivan Lendl as 'a haircut and a forehand', but the timing of his arrival on the scene was impeccable, with McEnroe and Connors on the way out, and the last three finals having all been disputed by Becker and Edberg. It had left a big gaping personality hole to fill, and boy, was Agassi up for that role.

Agassi was the teen phenomenon[xxi] who had crashed into tennis under the headline 'IMAGE IS EVERYTHING', the strapline in an ad campaign he starred in for Canon's new 'Rebel' cameras. The TV spot featured Agassi, The Rebel, doing rebellious things like wearing pink swimshorts, driving a jeep with one hand, not checking his mirrors when reversing, wearing shades indoors and just standing in Las Vegas by lots of neon signs, looking like trouble. He had already become a bit of a joke in the game, repeatedly losing Major finals, seriously under-performing when it came to the big stages and being more famous for his fluorescent pink lycra, stone-washed denim shorts and midriff-bearing t-shirts. The Las Vegan wore his hair in a long, dyed blonde mullet, which flew all over the place with his exaggerated two-handed turbo-game, giving him the appearance of someone living

on a trailer park playing swingball after downing five litres of Gatorade.

He finally rolled into SW19 in 1991 having avoided the All England Club for the last three years[xxii], citing its traditionalism and all-white dress code as solid reasons to stay away. He was the biggest pull in the men's game and the decision to play was met with a media barrage, mainly focused on what he might wear. The newspapers lapped it up, with headlines like 'AGASSI WILL BE ALL WHITE', which was quite funny, and 'MR CLEAN SHOWS HE IS NO PAIN IN THE AGASSI', which didn't really make sense[xxiii].

The Nevadan did not disappoint, hamming up the drama in interviews and coming out on the day looking like the bees knees in a pristine all-white exact replica of his normal attire, bringing a delighted roar from the crowd and worldwide fascination for the beaming, reborn star. By that night the newly converted, and increasingly excitable, Agassi would say:

'Wimbledon is something bigger than tennis. You walk out there and the classiness of the surroundings hits you. I have never enjoyed playing anywhere more.'

WIMBLEDON IS EVERYTHING™

CHURCH ON A SUNDAY

The weather had been awful pretty much all of the first week and with the tournament now days behind schedule, the Club did some grey-sky thinking and promptly announced that there would be a 'Middle Sunday', with all showcourt tickets priced at £10. They didn't normally play on the Middle Sunday, probably in order to make the second Sunday seem all the more special, a bit like *Chariots of Fire*, but without the religious angle.

On the subject of religion, I now had a job at the local Sutton Churches Tennis Club, situated opposite Sutton United Football Club, five miles, and a whole world, away from the AELTC. It was a slightly misleading name in that I never saw a single reference to God, and some of the language you'd hear during a Ladies' doubles club match would have made a vicar blush. As a classic suburban sporting institution it had a small clubhouse and bar, where the lingering smell of creosote hung in every corner, and a social notices board which advertised events from three summers ago.

As well as being an employee I also played my tennis there, recently scaling the dizzy heights by reaching the third round of an under-18 boys' singles. In the second round I beat a lad called Matt Little, who was a couple of years younger than me, but I knew well as our Mums were best pals and our families would holiday in Cornwall together. Matt was such a kind chap that he offered to help me get prepared for my third round match against the defending champion, and club chairman's son, Sebastian Bentley. I was 16, going on 11, whilst Sebastian Bentley was 17, worked in an office, drove a Rover, went out with a 21-year-old hairdresser and had a serve like Zivojinovic. Matt had me run some exercises in the tramlines and knocked up with me for half an hour. I remember coming in to the net and asking him, in the pro-style, to put some lobs up for smashes, and neither could he accurately achieve the lobs, nor could I hit a decent overhead smash.

The warm-up turned out to be longer than the match as I lost 6-0, 6-0, in a club record 29 minutes, winning an estimated four points, with three of them coming from Slobodan Sebastinovic's bored double faults, as he talked to his courtside hairdresser about whether or not they would drive to Brighton the next day. Matt would later go on to prove that you could only work with the talent in front of you as, in his long-term role as strength and conditioning coach for Andy Murray, he would be part of a team that (spoiler alert) won Wimbledon twice, the US Open, the Davis Cup and two Olympic gold medals.

The job I had taken on at Sutton Churches involved me rolling the shale courts before their club matches on a Saturday morning, and then returning at 5pm to roll them again until 7pm. It was the most ridiculously difficult and thankless job whose only perk was the vast collection of European tennis magazines in the head groundsman's shed, which featured saucy photos of German women in the shower.

By the time I got home that Saturday they were already showing footage of a 1.5-mile line and I couldn't believe that I had missed my chance to be a part of the carnival atmosphere. It looked electric on the TV the next day and even Gabriela Sabatini, not known for her frolicsome personality, gushed afterwards, 'It was great fun. I couldn't stop laughing.' This last claim wasn't strictly speaking true, as photographic evidence proves, but you could see what she was getting at. The overall atmosphere, and meritocratic ticketing, led Martina to sum up what everyone was thinking. 'They should do this every year,' she said. I thought they should do it every day.

TIME WAITS FOR NO BOY

On the Sunday afternoon Bally and I headed up to the beloved pavement, joining the increasingly loud bandwagon that was the Andre Agassi Show, watching him beat Jacco Eltingh in the fourth round the next day to a rapturous reception. He seemed to be revelling in this Wimblelove, playing the role of the loveable scamp, as opposed to the moody, brash brat he was viewed as everywhere else.

NOSTALGIA FREAK
I was actually struggling a little with the passing of the 80s baton, seeing my favourite international stars, male and female, fading away at the ends of their illustrious careers. For some reason it really affected me in a highly emotional way, on occasion more than it seemed to affect even them. I was therefore pleased/relieved to see Mac back in the quarter-finals, because it reminded me of being ten again. I was chronically nostalgic and already spent hours staring at the ceiling, pining for my youth. I was only 17.

SAME OLD, SAME OLD
In British 'hopes', Andrew Castle took it back to the playground when he got feisty with a young Goran Ivanisevic, doing gorilla impressions of the big man as the Brit went down in four sets. Some semblance of revenge was exacted when another 'home hope', world No.591 Nick Brown, in turn took Grumpy Goran down in four sets in the next round before politely exiting the day after, along with Jeremy Bates. I may have been going through changes, but British tennis wasn't.

ACQUIRED TASTE
There was a new German in town, and I lined right up behind Boris in not being entirely happy about it. Michael Stich turned up from pretty much nowhere[29], with a game so elegant and graceful it initially made Boris look like a Luddite. To make matters worse he only went and won the whole thing, beating Becker himself in the final and leaving me, and Boris, completely flummoxed. After shaking his fists at the sky and shouting 'I'm not enjoying this!' in German, Becker started bashing his head against the back canvas and at

---

29 Hamburg, in fact.

one point I was pretty sure that he was actually barking. Who was this guy, and why was he making BB do dog impressions?

Stich looked like a successful European businessman who drove an Audi and had a collection of tasteful brown leather jackets and one of those soft briefcases with a shoulder strap. He probably owned a pair of loafers and knew more than one way to do up a tie. His style was far too finessed for my teenaged palate – I just couldn't get my head round it. He was like a bowl of green and black olives; you wanted to like them, but deep down you really didn't understand them, find them in any way pleasing or crave them like you did Wotsits. Not that I want to liken the great Boris to a packet of cheesy puffs.

Ladies' Champion *Steffi Graf*
Gentlemen's Champion *Michael Stich*

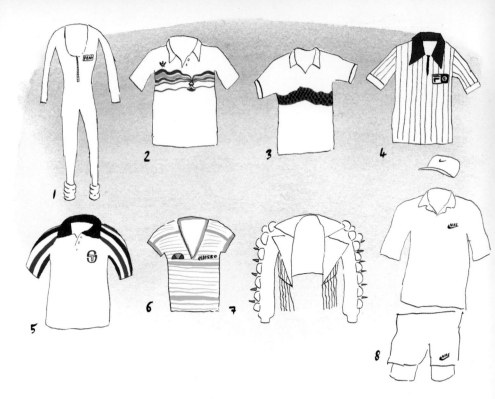

WHITE NOISE

Part 1

For a bunch of sportos only allowed to wear one colour, Wimbledon can boast a surprisingly eventful sartorial story …

1. Merry hell kicked off in 1985 after **Anne White** strode on to court in her Fame-inspired spandex Pony unitard and matching legwarmers. She was apparently baffled by the reaction, 'I had no idea it would be so controversial. It wasn't my intention, as I took my tracksuit off, for anyone to spill their strawberries and cream.' This is exactly the kind of thing people who are not baffled by the reaction say. Still, great name, great kit.

2. **Ivan Lendl**'s 'The Face'. Also known as The Wavy Face, or even The Cat's Face, this was a 1987 technicolour design classic created by adidas for Ivan Lendl, but worn by a number of players, including 'The Becker Wrecker' himself, Peter Doohan.

3. **John McEnroe**'s checkerboard Challenge Court shirt from '85 looked like something you used to get in one of those mod shops on Carnaby Street, before the iconic little avenue went all commercial. As if a strip had been ripped across the chest to show his rebellious inner ska beast.

4. The **Björn Borg** FILA Bj really was the crème de la Européene chic crème, selling for a whopping $70 even back then in 1977. A stretchy, gorgeous, thin cotton, an effortless design and a fit so slim that you had to be a tennis pro, or seriously malnourished, to get away with it. The shirt was so ubiquitous in the 70s country club scene of America that it is actually featured in the film *Caddyshack*. A little-known fact is that John McEnroe wore a version of it when playing at Wimbledon 1977 as a young qualifier.

5. The barber-shop sleeves and fiery red headband of **John McEnroe**'s 1980 final shirt contrasted perfectly with Borg in the classic above, in the match which was even a perfect sartorial face-off.

6. There is a naïve charm to both tennis in 1985 and the 'Club Tropicana' chic of the summer classics which Ellesse made for **Chris Evert**. Before they went rubbish and started selling velcro trainers in Sports Direct (see also Sergio Tacchini, and FILA), Ellesse were the Andrew to FILA's George.

7. **Bethanie Mattek-Sands** made pretty much sure of media attention with a selection of creatively stimulating outfits throughout the Noughties. The Urban-Rockabilly-Cowgirl-goes to-'Nam (she wore black war paint under her eyes) look from 2011 was probably her pinnacle.

8. **Andre Agassi**'s non-appearances at Wimbledon were well-documented, with many citing his dislike of the colour codes as the major stumbling block. When he finally made it in 1991, sporting a pristine white version of his day-glo outfits, it endeared him to every sports fan in the world. Including Steffi Graf.

THE APPLIANCE OF SCIENCE

On the first Monday the *Daily Mirror* dusted off the old Gruntometer and put it courtside for Monica Seles's first round match. She rarely registered 'above 65', which was apparently just the noise of a 'busy office'.

NATIONAL PLEASURE

A wildcard is a form of qualifying whereby your ranking is not high enough to get you into a big tournament automatically but gifts you a place in the main draw, thus avoiding the hassle of playing qualification rounds. They are normally used by tournaments to give to established players returning from injury, local talent needing a leg up or, in Wimbledon's case, complete no-hopers who are ranked about 900 in the world and haven't won a match anywhere since a junior doubles title at their club's summer fête. For these ones the 'wild' prefix should be replaced by 'Snowball-in-hell'. Incredibly, in 1992 three British Snowball-in-hell-Card entries came through their first round matches, a success on the home front which was greeted with national fervour in the papers; 'GREAT

BRITS FLY THE FLAG' and 'BATTLING BRITONS BLAZING A GLORY TRAIL', they roared[xxiv]. I could never quite understand why British success led to headlines which were always so militant and bombastic, and why we were always talking about flying these flags. But what the hell, I was going with it. It felt just like V-E Day. Probably.

Jeremy Bates had launched into the tournament somewhat emphatically by seeing off American No.7 seed, and a former French Open champion, Michael Chang, in the first round, then coming through a five-setter in the third round against the misleadingly-named Frenchman, Thierry Champion. The momentum was growing, marking the first time in my life that we had a British player actually in the competition past the middle weekend. To top it all Jeremy had provided the perfect 'plucky Brit' story to go with it.

FORGIVE & FORGET

Bates, in his humble and self-effacing British way, had actually arranged his stag party for the second week of Wimbledon[xxv], a tournament he must have entered with a vague plan of winning, even if knowing he probably wouldn't. It did seem a shade pessimistic – he was a professional tennis player. The actual concept of some form of success in the tournament shouldn't have completely evaded him. Heineken ran an advert with the consumer-confusing tagline of, 'Heineken refreshes the Brits other beers cannot reach'. Was Bates drinking beer throughout his matches? Was this actually allowed? Was he getting in practice for the stag do? The bookies even joined in by 'slashing' the odds on a Briton lifting the title from a snowball-in-hell-ish 1,000-1 to the not entirely dissimilar 500-1.

Sadly Bates need not have worried about moving the festivities, as he hit the wall in the fourth round, going down to No.9 seed Guy Forget in five thrilling sets, having held a match point in the fourth, or a 'stag point', as I liked to call it.

The game was also memorable for the fact that Monsieur Forget, already the best cartoon caricature of a Frenchman ever seen, in his Lacoste whites and general pantomime Pierrot mannerisms, actually wore a knotted blue neckerchief under his shirt. He might as well have slicked his hair back, covered his face in white make-up and mimed his service action. I think the kind Gallic victor actually said, 'Bof!', as he generously consoled Bates at the net after their five-set epic *bataille*.

FROM A LAND DOWN UNDER

We were back on the streets on the Friday night, as were my Mum and her SLQA chums, positioned a few hundred metres away. The Australian soap opera *Neighbours* was in full effect during this period and my life was still (pathetically, immaturely) affected by the 5.35pm slot and the endless array of tanned Australian beauties on the show. Having grown out of Charlene and Jane, I fostered a particular fondness for bubbly blonde Bronwyn Davies, played by the actress Rachel Friend. As we stood in The Queue that evening, surveying the hordes leaving after a day inside, I stared in utter disbelief as I saw none other than Ms Friend, with a microphone and crew, interviewing my Mum and her chums.

She was working for an Australian TV channel presenting a feature on the makeshift campsite when, unbeknownst to me, one of the SLQA ladies informed the star that her friend's son 'fancied her'. I was dragged over, feeling like a massive plum, and forced in to awkward chit chat with the soap star of my dreams, as we had our photo taken together. This led to a conversation so dry that at one point I asked her if she had 'enjoyed the flight over'. In the photos you can see how bashful I am by the fact that I put my arm around her handbag rather than her shoulder. Still, it was easily the most exciting thing to happen to me since chumming it up with Boris Becker in a car park.

A LAST HURRAH

A McEnroe story was gathering pace in 1992 and, after the Connors heroics (and some of the foulest on-court outbursts ever witnessed) from the previous year's US Open, when he rode to the semis on a nostalgic tidal wave of crowd emotion, people were beginning to talk up Mac's chances. McEnroe was unseeded so his draw had him up against big names from the early rounds, seeing him beat Pat Cash in a five-set classic early on. He then comfortably beat the No.9 seed, Guy Forget, in the quarters, displaying the full 80s swagger and touch, with less of the grumbling and menacing self-immolation. Sadly, by the time he reached the semis he had pushed his 33-year-old body as far as it would go and, facing an Andre Agassi very much in 'the zone', and building on his momentum from the previous year's crowd love-wave, Mac went down in straight sets. There was no shame in that and he could even manage one last veiled swipe at his vintage nemesis when he said, 'I used to think that Jimmy Connors was the best service-returner we'll ever see – but Andre has taken it to a new level,' with no hint of a smirk.

AGASSI COMPLETES HIS RESURRECTION

Agassi went on to win his first ever Major on the Sunday, collapsing in disbelief on the grass, a surface on which every expert said he could never win. The vanquished Ivanisevic, arguably the greatest server of all time, had notched 37 aces (the same number as Agassi had in the whole tournament) but couldn't get past the incredible returns of his inspired opponent. The Croatian still won a lot of new fans by climbing over the net, hugging the disbelieving victor and generally behaving like a total gent in defeat.

It was one of sport's great stories; the flashy Vegas kid who is marketed like a star before he wins anything, dismisses Wimbledon for its crushingly traditional approach and old-fashioned grass, before finally showing up, super late for the party, and making everyone fall in love with him. He was Kevin Bacon in *Footloose*, the 'Big city kid in a small town', 'they said he'd never win … He knew he had to.' Later that night he attended the traditional black tie Champions' dinner, and no doubt enjoyed the photo with the Belle of Wimbledon, Ladies' Champion Steffi Graf[30].

MEMORIES, LIKE THE CORNERS OF MY MIND

Schedule delays meant that No.1 Court was opened on the Monday (for free), where they played the men's doubles final in front of a packed crowd of boisterous fans. Peter Fleming, who won seven Majors as McEnroe's doubles partner, once said: 'The best doubles pair in the world is John McEnroe … and anyone,' so in theory it didn't matter who was standing alongside him. €uroMan Michael Stich took on the anyone role that day, as they came through in a five-setter, ending in fitting drama, 19-17 in the fifth. McEnroe himself served it

---

30 A story which would become more significant seven years later when Graf and Agassi first started hitting together and then started hitting on each other. They are, at the time of writing, happily married with two children.

out in style, in his last-ever professional match at Wimbledon, as the crowd gave him the send-off he deserved (and secretly craved), on the courts where he had once screamed, 'I'm so disgusting, you shouldn't watch. Everybody leave!'[xxvi]

As Sue Barker rolled the titles that night they played a compilation of McEnroe's halcyon days against the poignant notes of Barbra Streisand's excruciatingly sentimental 1973 song 'The Way We Were'. I was a sucker for some overt sporting sentiment, hated to see a changing of the guard and therefore found myself sitting sobbing on the front room floor. I was 18.

DREAM OF A MAN

The commentator, Dan Maskell, AKA the 'Voice of tennis', was a 24-carat stalwart of the British game who came from a working-class background but had coached members of the Royal Family and had also attended every single day of The Championships since 1929. He was a firm 'national treasure' for his charming views of an unfolding match, delivered in a reassuringly gentle, measured and easy-going voice. His distinctive style was best articulated in his uniquely delivered catchphrases; 'Quite extraordinary', said as if leaning back in an armchair, 'Dream of a backhand' and, of course, the emphatic, 'Oh, I say … ', after which he then didn't actually say anything. This was to be his last Wimbledon as he passed away later in the year.

Ladies' Champion *Steffi Graf*
Gentlemen's Champion *Andre Agassi*

IS A CHANGE AS GOOD AS A REST?

With a stinker of a first year at university in Nottingham over, I was packed up and back in London by 10pm on the first Monday and also back in The Queue, my other London residence, by 8.00 the next morning. On arrival, I already noticed a major difference as the first 200 metres of space, the pavement I thought of as 'My Pavement[31]' was very much full. I followed the line further and further into the distance and finally took my place, number 300-and-something, halfway to Southfields tube station.

The pavement here in the +300 Ghetto was about a metre wide and I was considerably more than a metre tall, with no roadside barriers to protect you and nowhere to hang your tarpaulin. To make matters worse all around me were people having fun in large groups of friends – drinking heavily and spilling out into the road like we were at the Notting Hill Carnival. Where were Derek and Cynthia? Where was David The Kindly Steward? Who was going to share food with me? Having spent an awkward year at university feeling excluded socially, this was not my ideal evening.

---

31 Merton Council take a different view.

At about 2am the Australians to the left of me finally stopped finding each other hilarious and the South Africans to the right of me got so drunk that they couldn't hit their bongo drum any more. I lay with my legs dangling precariously from the thigh down over the kerb and into the busy road, dropping off to sleep for a full three minutes before a souped-up Austin Maestro almost sliced my lower limbs off as it screeched past, horn blowing wildly. By 6am I had not slept at all and was almost completely out on my feet, staggering around like a bleary-eyed boxer in a surreal dreamscape. The only thing I remember was a peaceful-looking lady sitting near me who looked up from her paper and for no apparent reason said, 'Are the top players called "seeds" because they are the ones most likely to "flower"?' There exists the possibility that I was hallucinating.

A WOMAN IN LOVE

The next day was remarkable for a number of reasons:

(1) Both matches went to five sets and were absolute corkers.

(2) My seat was right by the Andre Agassi team's box, which that day included songstress Barbra Streisand, inexplicably dressed as a sailor, even sporting the captain's hat. I genuinely think she might have got Wimbledon confused with Henley. I only really knew her as a late-night favourite of my Dad's, a man so lacking in musical taste that he thought ELO were better than The Beatles. I could also never work out why she appeared in some shops as 'Easy Listening', when I always found it particularly hard.

Throughout the match I couldn't stop looking over at her, it seemed so utterly bonkers and weird that this icon was here, as his (alleged) girlfriend and who, at 51, was 30 years older than Agassi's long-term girlfriend, Wendi, spelled with an 'i'.

Poor old Wendi had flown in for a 'secret rendezvous' with her star-struck fella, starting off negotiations by 'chucking Andre's Streisand CDs out of their limousine window.'[32] Well, you would definitely start there.

(3) I was so chronically tired that by the third set of Becker v Stich I actually thought I had contracted myalgic encephalomyelitis, or ME as it is more commonly known. At one point I actually fell fast asleep on the shoulder of the old dear sitting next to me, making me look like an enormous oddball.

Boris came through an incredibly salty match with Stich, which saw them both going off for a loo break before the fifth set, with rumours of a bit of verbal argy-bargy at the urinals. Petros 'Pete' Sampras overcame Agassi in five pulsating sets, with Andre stating 'I'll win it next year', delivered in such a matter-of-fact, 'I'll pick up the milk on the way home, love' tone that everyone believed him[33]. Petros went on to beat Boris in the semis and win his first Wimbledon against Jim Courier in the final. It all felt strangely empty, in part as I had grown up watching tennis players with rainbow-coloured personalities and Sampras simply paled in comparison, seeming to me to be all substance and no style.

IT'S ALL IN THE HEAD

With academic reading complete for now I decided to tackle W. Timothy Gallwey's seminal *The Inner Game of Tennis* the next day in The Queue. The tome was considered to be the bible of tennis psychology and I had been recommended it in an attempt to work out why my own game would often collapse in a matter of seconds. The American golfer, Gary Player's, famous maxim that, 'The more I practise, the luckier

---

32 According to the *Sunday Mirror*.
33 He didn't.

I get', seemed to be working in the exact inverse for me, as the book's focus on us all having two inner personalities succeeded largely in making me bipolar. My forehand remained wayward.

OVER A BRIT QUICK

In British news our wildcard Chris Bailey took huge-serving No.5 seed Goran Ivanisevic to five jangly sets in the second round before bowing out, while Jeremy Bates failed to repeat his heroics of the previous year, losing in the first round. 'MR NICE TURNS NASTY', shouted the tabloids as Sampras's 'F-WORD TANTRUM'[xxvii] shocked the British fans, who were only indulging in a bit of light-hearted extreme nationalism, in his match against last-Brit-standing Andrew Foster. Sampras finished by smashing the ball into the crowd and shouting some unmentionables. Talk about kick a nation when we're down.

IF YOU CAN KEEP YOUR HEAD … OH, BOLLOCKS

Women's tennis was considerably more interesting than the men's in 1993, both on and off the court. After the horrors of Monica Seles's stabbing during a match in Hamburg in April, Steffi Graf and Jana Novotna served up one of the most outlandish slices of tennis drama that I had ever seen on the court[34].

Eighth-seeded Novotna, of the Czech Republic, performed what sports folk refer to as a 'choke', or an almighty wobble when the endline, and glory, is in plain sight, often with a great lead being squandered. It is referred to in everyday life as a 'balls up'.

---

34 Part One. Brilliantly, this Shakespearean tragedy had a second act – see 1998.

Graf was the No.1 and overwhelming favourite to take another title, winning a tie-break first set before Novotna had hit a purple patch in the second, taking it 6-1, and was now cruising at 4-1 and 40-30 up in the decider, with a point for a 5-1 lead. The TV commentary had legendary Wimbledon voice John Barrett, like a sporting Michael Fish, stating confidently: 'I think the belief is there. At moments like this in the past she has tended to choke on her leads. But I don't think it's going to happen today.'

Novotna's exaggerated serving action and soaring ball-toss made you feel as if you were watching a high-wire act at the best of times, and this was crytallised at exactly that moment when she ballooned a second serve about four feet long. Then she tonked a volley about twice that length out … and barely won any more points as her whole psyche appeared to collapse before our eyes. Graf, wearing the faintly disbelieving look of someone who was pretty much in her taxi home about five minutes before, didn't need to do much other than just exist, and wrapped the set up 6-4, for the loss of no more games. She admitted afterwards that she thought she had lost the match, which is a rare thing for a serial winner like Steffi to concede.

On receiving her runner's-up plate from the ever-sympathetic Duchess of Kent, Jana briefly held it together and then crumbled almost instantly, balling her eyes out like a kid in primary school losing it with a teacher when they fluff their lines in the nativity play. She rested her head on the Duchess's shoulder and seemed to stay there for an eternity. 'One day you will do it … I know you will,' the Duchess is supposed to have said to spark the waterworks.

I thought Jana might have been better off with some tough love, along the lines of, 'You pillock Jana, you absolute jelly-limbed pillock. You'll probably never get the chance to

do that again. You were about to beat Steffi Freakin' Graf, you wally. Go and beat yourself over the back with birch branches for a good 30 strokes.' Some of the headline writers tried to be reasonable – 'NOVOTNA FINDS ROYAL SHOULDER TO CRY ON' and 'CRYING GAME' – some didn't ... 'VOT A CHOKER!'[xxviii]

Ladies' Champion *Steffi Graf*
Gentlemen's Champion *Pete Sampras*

QUEEN AND COUNTRY

I was back on the courts of south-west London in June having got my student life together, growing my hair long to prove the point, so sporting the attitude of a young McEnroe, twinned with the bobbed coiffure of a mid-period Hana Mandlikova[xxix]. At Queen's I watched with a mixture of incredulity and irritation as Jeremy Bates beat Boris Becker in the second round, knowing full well that the Brit wouldn't go on to win it. Fred Perry, writing for the *Daily Telegraph*, acknowledged the now 60 years it had been since he had won it himself, offering up hopefully, and entirely unconvincingly, 'It is staggering to think that no British male has been able to do it since ... Let's hope someone does something spectacular.' Like possibly reach the second week.

GUERRILLERA HEROICA

Back in SW19, The Queue was bursting at the seams, but still seemed less 'other' than it had the previous year, as I managed to take back my Church Road bedroom when camping out on the first Sunday. In The Queue next to me was a fully committed, almost militant, lady called Helen who wasted no time in sharing her opinions on a broad range of subjects, informing me, almost threateningly, 'I do like to chinwag, young man.' Back then we didn't have smartphones to hide behind, so you had to actually talk to people in your proximity. Citizen Helen was from Oxford and seemed mightily enraged by what she described as 'the so-called[35] "new fans" of tennis' who are 'only here to see the stars'. She also had a bee in her bonnet about people who acquired tickets through the ballot, calling them, 'opportunists', adding, with an actual hiss, 'Pre-paid is not real tennis.' She was like the human equivalent of a smacked bottom. I suggested that these ballot winners had just applied for tickets like everyone else, and they were hardly sacrificing any ethical principles by posting their self-addressed envelope.

Later in the afternoon I was genuinely concerned when she told me, 'I have one dog, he is a Shih Tzu, called Buster Mottram.' Not only is it strange to give a dog two names (especially when one is a surname), and strange to name a dog after a well-known person, but it is also decidedly strange to name him after that particular man. Mottram was a former British No.1, who was shunned by the tennis world after he expressed his support for the National Front and the political ideology of big fat fascist, Enoch Powell.

Helen listened to her portable radio annoyingly loud all evening, including a play which was set during a whist drive in Nuneaton and an episode of *Desert Island Discs*[xxx] in which I had not heard of one of the songs the castaway nuclear physicist chose. It was a chilly night and at one point she told me that she had 'her winter drawers on', which was not information I wanted to be party to.

Later on I was so bored that I drew up a list of what songs The Queue would choose if it were stranded on the desert island and came up with 'Here I Go Again' by Whitesnake,

---

35 By her.

'I'm Still Waiting' by Diana Ross, 'I'm So Tired' by The Beatles and 'Helen, The Angry Middle-Class Racist Next Door' by Me.

The next day I watched Boris, ranked down at a lowly No.7, beat a German I had never heard of but I spent most of my time trying to not talk to hate-filled Helen. This was particularly tricky as she was sitting next to me. At one point she reached into her bag to show me a toilet roll, informing me that she always brought her own into the grounds in case of 'disaster'.

GROUNDHOG BATES

Incredibly, Jeremy Bates repeated his heroics of 1992 by again reaching the fourth round, even more incredibly hitting the same Guy Forget wall. He went down in a respectable four sets to the Gallic national heartbreaker, and lovable French caricature. Fred Perry called Bates a 'standard-bearer', which, if taken in the non-military sense, meant someone who was leading a group of people who were all having similar ideas. I really couldn't see these other British people having the idea of progressing through to the second week of Wimbledon.

LADIES FIRST

It was only in 1994, somewhat incredibly, that ball girls were first allowed to assist in the operation of the Centre and No.1 Court scoreboards, a feat they managed with aplomb. On the playing side it was once again left to the ladies to throw up the more interesting stories around The Championships, kicking off on day one when the defending champion and No.1 seed Steffi Graf astonishingly crashed out in the first round to American Lori McNeil.

Martina, at the tender age of 37, ground her way back to the final, where she lost to Spanish star Conchita Martinez, but saw her popularity with the crowd reach an all-time high. She was now one of the elite group of sportspeople who have reached such iconic status in their field that they can be referred to by just their first name. See also; Tiger, Steffi, Björn, Boris, Diego, Pelé, Roger, Billie Jean, Ayrton. Being an icon certainly helps this process, as does having a really unique name which hardly anyone else has. Or being a raging maniac like OJ. Or Lance.

TAEDIUM VITAE

The final felt like a low point for men's tennis with the giants of the game, Sampras and Ivanisevic, hammering down a total of 42 aces on to the soft grass[xxxi] in a largely tactical battle in which rallies were kept to a minimum and the main source of interest came from Ivanisevic's occasionally erratic temperament. I felt genuinely concerned that Pistol Pete's domination was beginning to kill the game off as a spectacle, his service action making him look like a humanised tennis ball machine. There was a lot to admire in the Californian; this almost perfect serving style and delivery (in which it was said he had something approaching 100% belief and confidence), his cool and calm temperament and his (normally) impeccable manners, but crikey he was hard work to get excited about.

Ladies' Champion *Conchita Martinez*
Gentlemen's Champion *Pete Sampras*

FAIRE LA QUEUE

1995 was the year that wasn't, in that I wasn't in The Queue at Wimbledon at all, although I was still sleeping relatively rough. On the first day of the tournament I was working as a beach seller in St Tropez, dragging a giant icebox up and down the sweltering sand with almost no selling success, on one day managing to sell minus one cans of Orangina. I was so poor that I lived in a collapsed tent which was essentially a plastic bag, on the fringes of a campsite, where there were so many insects that the sadistic owner would let you stay for just two francs a night and sit watching in glee as spiders the size of dinner plates approached you from all sides.

L'Equipe, the brilliant French sports newspaper, at the time cost about the same as half a croissant, putting it out of my price range, but there was a small café on my hellish campsite where they generously put the paper out in the morning with a giant 'Le Snacky' logo stuck on it, so no-one would dare steal it. From *le 26 Juin* to *le 9 Juillet* I pilfered that paper every single day, sneaking in from the east and hiding it under my towel before darting in to the bamboo shoots and devouring it, along with a hearty breakfast of last night's leftover ready salted crisps and some warm water from the tap in the communal toilets. It was the only way I could stay in touch with the action. Whilst Wimbledon had recently launched a website, possibly the first major sports event in the UK to do it on this scale, the internet was far from being in common use at this point and there was virtually no way of 'getting online'. London seemed so bloody far away[36].

BACK TO THE OLD POUTINE

With the British men's game at an all-time low word got out earlier in the year that big-serving Canadian beefcake, Greg Rusedski, might be making the 'lifestyle decision' to switch nationalities and play for Great Britain. The 21-year-old could boast both a British mother plus a British girlfriend (who he supposedly met when she was a ball girl in a junior tournament he was playing in), although only the former qualified him for the switch. You couldn't snog your way to a passport – a proud stance that Great Britain still stands behind today. He duly rocked up at the All England Club, grinning incredibly broadly and sporting a Union Jack bandana, like all good patriots. He then lost in straight sets to Pete Sampras, like all good patriots. Losing to Sampras would become a much-loved British tradition over the years, like morris dancing, or cheese-rolling.

THERE ARE NO ACCIDENTS

In the year that Fred Perry passed away the Brits were back in town, and this time they meant serious business. New British star and 'Possible Future Wimbledon Champion™', Tim Henman, came from a family with bona fide tennis DNA, boasting grandparents who had played on Wimbledon's hallowed lawns and a great grandmother who was possibly the

---

36 At 900 miles door-to-door, arguably it actually was.

first woman to serve over-arm, back in 1901. His elegant game, combined with a gritty streak, proved on his slog round the satellite circuit, augered well for the nation's hopes. This was his second Wimbledon and, while he was patriotically ousted by Sampras in the second round of the singles, he partnered up with previous Possible Future Wimbledon Champion™, Jeremy Bates, in the doubles to take on Jeff Tarango and Henrik Holm.

Leading two sets to one and angered by a net cord, hot-headed Henman smashed a ball in anger, straight into the head of 16-year-old ball girl Caroline Hall, who collapsed to the floor, holding her parietal ridge in agony. Like a confused yet determined boxer, Hall then staggered to her feet only to teeter off court in tears, clutching an ice pack. An angry Alan Mills, the tournament referee, with the incendiary Tarango standing unsympathetically behind making a lot of shocked faces, had no option. Henman thus became the first-ever player to be kicked out of Wimbledon. Tarango, gasping theatrically, said: 'With the speed of the ball it could have

killed her,' going through a full repertoire of slightly camp overreactions.

In the coming days Henman consoled himself with over 750 'morale-boosting letters', which he had received from the sympathetic British public, stating that 'not one of them was negative'.

I wondered what on earth people were writing …

'Dear Tim,

She deserved it. You're the best.

You should smash more balls at the little blighters.

Regards,

The Butterworths, Burford.'

EFFIN AND JEFFIN

Four days later, Wimbledon's favourite hot-blooded Californian wind-up merchant, Jeff Tarango[37], was playing singles on an outside court and getting a bit stroppy with the crowd. Caroline Hall, of all people, the 'trouble-will-find-you' ball girl, had just been tasked with taking him over some bananas from the main office, which would prove somewhat appropriate. Tarango first told the crowd to 'Shut up', then excoriated the umpire Bruno Rebeuh after numerous over-rules against him and then stomped off court, wailing, 'I'm not playing anymore!', thereby forfeiting the match.

His similarly hot-headed wife, a you-couldn't-make-her-up French lady called Benedicte, decided to add a final act, slapping Rebeuh a couple of times in the face for good Gallic parody measure. Tim Henman, busy reading his letters at home, must have been loving it. When later asked to explain

---

37 Once the bright young thing of junior American tennis, who had a massive winning record against Sampras at that level.

his wife's behaviour Tarango replied, 'Well, she's French, and I'm still learning the culture,' adding, with no hint of irony, 'you know … Women are emotional.'

The *Sunday Mirror* screamed 'You've been Tarangoed!', a reference to a popular recent advert for Tango fizzy drinks in which a funny man in a rubber orange suit slapped members of the public in the face for seemingly no reason, with the strapline, 'You know when you've been Tango'd.' It was almost prophetic.

BLOOD IS THICKER THAN BARLEY WATER

It is one of Wimbledon's top traditions that 'Robinsons Barley Water' is still its official drink, and I for one was pleased to see it still holding its own on the courts. It puts everyone in mind of sports days, plastic cups and being told to 'drink slowly', a constant presence for 80-odd years, since Eric Smedley Hodgson started mixing lemon, barley, water and sugar right there in the SW19 changing rooms. It still sits defiantly by the umpire's chair now, barely touched but calmly staring down the players' isotonic energy waters laced with the dew of Himalayan mountain grass.

In the Ladies' event the main news I could glean was that scorching on-court temperatures had led to a female player collapsing with heat exhaustion. Despite attempts to revive her with glasses of barley water and energetic fanning she appeared to be out cold. Or hot. Unsurprisingly she turned out to be British.

Ladies' Champion *Steffi Graf*
Gentlemen's Champion *Pete Sampras*

COOL BRITANNIA

It was the year of the 'Lad', a kind of celebration of shouting and throwing your arms up in the air a lot, which was swiftly followed by the female equivalent, the 'Ladette'. These two factions together created an exciting new youth movement, 'Cool Britannia', which was talked about all over the world, but had actually been brought into the public arena when Ben & Jerry's launched a strawberry-based ice cream with that name the year before.

Our hedonistic music ruled the airwaves, our anarchic films were everywhere, our fashion was really, really fashionable and our prime minister played the electric guitar. Our pop tunes were also at the top again, particularly in the form of The Spice Girls, a five-woman united attack on the senses screaming for girl power and kicking down social barriers along the way. Euro '96, the European Football Championships, was played in England for the first time and we had both a great manager and a team to match. By the time we got to the Sunday before Wimbledon the nation was singing together for the first time in years. Surely now was the time for our tennis players to rule Wimbledon?

CARRY ON CAMPING

In British news Jeremy Bates went out in the first round, and announced that it was his last tilt. He had been a proud flag-bearer[38] in a very lean time, even if the headline, 'PARTY IS FINALLY OVER FOR BATES'[xxxii], suggested that 'the party' had all been somewhat more of a ride than a couple of fourth rounds. Still, beggars and choosers and all that. Tim Henman, on the other hand, was starting to look like something approaching the real deal, already beating top 30 players with regularity.

Ms Caroline Hall was back in the news when she wished Henman luck, telling the journalist, with a strange air of mystic authority, that he would 'go a long way ... if it's not this year it will be soon'. On the Wednesday I found myself in The Queue next to a grown man wearing a home-made t-shirt emblazoned with the word 'Timbledon'. He had travelled up from Devon, clearly drunk on the excitement that Henman was generating, as he informed me that 'it was just like Beatlemania'. Based on the lack of screaming girls, Henman not being about to break America and the fact that this guy was about 19, the opinion just didn't stand up for me.

He also informed me knowingly that Henman would be 'bigger than Gazza' and that 'the Queen will give the country the week off if Henman wins it'. I questioned this, enquiring how that would play out with hospitals, the police, teachers and Marks & Spencers, but he remained adamant. The next day I found myself sitting three seats away from Timbledon on Centre Court and he absolutely cracked up laughing, like doubled up, when a little bird repeatedly flew across the

---

38 This military thing is easy to drop into.

baseline and caused a pause in play. That evening, in one of my fondest Wimbledon memories, the grounds stayed open as we watched England play Germany on the big screen on the hill. We lost, naturally.

Henman went on to reach the quarter-finals, going down in straight sets to amiable American No.13 seed, Todd Martin, while new Brit fave, Grinnin' Greg Rusedski, having enjoyed getting all the attention the previous year, could not repeat his success when getting a bit less of it, going down without a murmur in the second round.

COMMISERATIONS, NO JUBILATIONS
When the inevitable rains came Wimbledon experienced the first of many decidedly British moments that summer. Much like the mythologised 'Summer of Love' in 1967, 'Cool Britannia' embraced psychedelia in its poppiest form, just like The Beatles et al had 31 years earlier. This was most clearly seen in the form of the British Elvis-Alike, Sir Cliff Richard, who took the mic in the Royal Box on one day of particularly torrential rain. He had been 'persuaded' into singing his 60s hits 'Summer Holiday', 'Bachelor Boy' and 'Congratulations', with Martina leading an all-star female clapping chorus, to a crowd of utterly bemused tennis fans, myself included. It was claimed to have 'recreated the spirit of the Blitz' (Cliff's own words), but felt like the most depressing ever wet weekday at Butlins for some kind of Sixties Memories gang show. It also guaranteed the fact that every single time Cliff was shown on telly at Wimbledon (i.e. every year) the commentator would remind us all of the impromptu singalong.

OH, I SAY!
Also known as 'The Day Benny Hill Came To The All England Club'. Melissa Johnson looked like a rather prim

and proper young student who had probably been beavering away all year on a history degree at Durham, now working at The Championships to earn money for a summer trip to Thailand. Just before the Gentlemen's showpiece event between unlikely finalists Richard Krajicek and MaliVai Washington, she grabbed her moment of sporting glory with aplomb. Running on to court completely starkers except for a tiny maid's apron, the joyful nudist got a priceless smile from the two men stood at the net before jiggling on to the Royal Box where, to everyone's surprise, the Dukes and Duchesses, and even a slightly random vicar, all seemed to find the whole thing terribly amusing. MaliVai Washington returned to the baseline and lifted up his shirt to rapturous applause, while back in the Royal Box the 17-year-old Lord Frederick Windsor sat beaming, no doubt thinking that an afternoon out with the Olds had just got decidedly more interesting. It was easily the most exciting thing I had seen on Centre Court since Barbra Streisand dropped anchor in '93.

Even the Club itself later joined in the fun when it issued a particularly appropriate, and terribly British, statement regarding the streaker. Barely disguising a snigger, it read:

'Whilst we do not wish to condone the practice, it did at least provide some light amusement for our loyal and patient supporters, who have had a trying time during the recent bad weather.'[xxxiii]

It would prove to be just about the most interesting moment of the afternoon as Krajicek cruised past a 'just-happy-to-be-there' Washington who, still stuck on Ms Johnson rather than his straight sets defeat, excitedly commented afterwards: 'I look over and see this streaker. She lifted up the apron and she was smiling at me. I got flustered and three sets later I was gone; that was pretty funny.'

I don't know if it was 'funny', losing so comfortably in a Wimbledon final, but A Club-condoned Strip Show and a loser's cheque for £196,250? How very 1996.

Ladies' Champion *Steffi Graf*
Gentlemen's Champion *Richard Krajicek*

AT THE DOUBLE

Before the Brits could 'STORM IN TO BATTLE' a serious spanner was thrown into the 'Rule Britannia' fever sweeping the nation when it was discovered that double the amount of strawberries being sold in SW19 were not British, but Dutch, who could supply bigger, glossier, sexier berries which were twice as quick to pick. They were actually 'Double', these Dutch. Not only did they have a male singles champion, but now the Dutch were beating us at strawberries?

STICK IN THE MUD

Bad weather warnings were not an uncommon occurrence when it came to the 'world's most famous sporting event almost always affected by rain' and sure enough the nay-sayers were proved right as the ghastly climate hit straight off the bat, increasing the now deafening demand for a roof on Centre Court. The rains came down, Glastonbury was nicknamed 'Mudstock' (again) and a load of papers ran the headline 'SWIMBLEDON'.

My queuing experience during this wettest first week ever was remarkable for a bizarre meeting with three fascinating

Bulgarian women about halfway down Church Road. They referred to themselves as 'serious Navratilova fans', which I had already guessed, based on their Martina '84 spikey blonde mullet cuts and matching shell suits. I was daydreaming[39] and hadn't noticed that the people in front (the aforementioned three ladies) had moved on, leaving a large gap. In my haste I jogged along the muddy verge to catch up, inadvertently placing both my feet firmly in the middle of one of those spiteful square plastic straps they use to tie up bundles of newspapers.

This is a foolish move so screamingly obvious that it is like slipping on a banana skin, or having an anvil fall on you, which are only supposed to happen in cartoons, and not in real life. In fact, one lunchtime at uni I did watch in disbelief as my friend Neil actually slipped on a real-life banana skin and dropped his tray of sausage, chips and beans – that was 80p he'd never get back[40]. The strap brought me to the ground like a tackle round the knees from Jonah Lomu, although the rest of The Queue saw no one else around, and me lying prostrate in the mud, as though I had just thrown myself there for no reason.

The kind ladies helped me up as I lay face down, terribly winded, excruciatingly embarrassed and gasping for breath. Despite a forecast of thunderstorms, I had come dressed for a day at a country garden party, my paper-thin white sackcloth trousers now completely destroyed. One of the group kindly offered me a plastic mac and even helped dress my forehead, which was oozing blood where I had face-planted the steel peg holding the matted temporary pathway down. I must have looked a wretched sight; bleeding, covered in mud, wrapped

---

39 Recurrent theme, and a lost art. I blame mobile phones.
40 I also once saw a kid throw an eppy in the street by a drain as his embarrassed Mum explained to me, non-ironically, that he had 'lost his marbles'.

in plastic and wearing see-through trousers, being helped along by three petite, slightly concerned Navratilov-alikes.

POETS' CORNER

Back on site the All England Club installed a new board (replacing a very old one) above the players' entrance to Centre Court, featuring a quotation from Rudyard Kipling's poem, *If*, 'If you can meet with Triumph and Disaster, and treat those two imposters just the same.' I think the modern rewrite of the poem's opening is more accurate in the modern game.

> *'If you can keep your head while all around you are losing theirs ... there exists the possibility that you have not grasped the severity of the situation.'*

One assumed that they chose the quote either (a) because tennis truly is a game of inner mental turmoil or (b) to have one more dig at John McEnroe.

'SPECTATORS MUST BE DRESSED IN SUITABLE TENNIS ATTIRE THAT IS ALMOST ENTIRELY COVERED IN UNION JACKS'

Middle Sunday was back, by popular, or meteorological, demand and I joined the crowds on the street, many of whom were wearing Union Jack tennis ball earrings and plastic strawberry-themed headwear, to go in and witness Tim Henman playing out a nail-biter with Paul Haarhuis. This euphoric victory (and the earrings) led to another slew of articles about the 'Real Fans'; a phenomenon which was becoming a shade tiresome. I really was a 'Real Fan' but didn't feel the wearing of a Union Jack wig was necessary to prove that point. A large proportion of the sartorially jingoistic jokers Real Fans also seemed to cheer a hell of a lot of Haarhuis's errors, even Henman seeming a shade embarrassed by the whole thing. For that reason, 'Henmania' felt a bit like an unrequited love match, or a very strange form of 'manic disorder'.

GAME CHANGER

The new No.1 Court had unofficially kicked off earlier in the month when an edition of BBC TV's religious Sunday singalong programme, *Songs of Praise*, was recorded there. Any kind of blessing for British success would have been gratefully received, although rumours that an optimistic version of Christian hymn 'Morning Has Broken' was performed by the Band of the RAF Regiment as 'Henman Has Broken' were unproven.

The new stadium itself, with its faultless views and wide gangways, highlighted how much Wimbledon was changing, and, being a nostalgia freak, I wasn't sure I liked it. I already missed the old No.1, with its giant slab of a stand, its cool walk way along one side, its weird slatted seats that hurt your bum and the fact that you could hear the intrusive roar from Centre Court next door.

One of the side effects of the new court was the giant screen that was installed across the western edge, facing 'the hill'. I knew it was going to become 'a thing' when someone, no one knows who, first referred to it as 'Henman Hill', as this was where the Brit fans would gather if they couldn't get on to the showcourt to see him play live. To be fair we had been so starved of success that the slightest glimmer of hope was understandably treated as a cue for a national gathering, and there was emotional safety in numbers. This grassy knoll would actually go on to be almost personified as a national treasure, much like Helen Mirren, Morecambe & Wise or *The Antiques Roadshow.*

Tim knocked out reigning champion Krajicek, prompting a headline 'BRITAIN IN A HEN-ZY AS OUR HERO MARCHES ON TOWARDS THE TITLE'[xxxiv] but, like Rusedski, crashed out in the quarters. In Henman's case he fell to an inspired Micha€l Stich, in full €uro-business mode, all Germanic and €fficacious.

IN A TWIST

The BBC allegedly banned 'knicker shots' of the Ladies, thereby giving all the newspapers a chance to show a plethora of pics of tennis players flashing their knickers. A 16-year-old Russian called Anna Kournikova, who had been inappropriately nicknamed 'Lolita' by the press, announced her arrival, even though it had been common knowledge in tennis circles that she was so bankable that she'd signed a long-term contract with the agency IMG at the age of ten.

She played like a dream, smiled like a goofy teen and went all the way to the semis on a wave of youthful exuberance.

On the other half of the draw Jana Novotna reached her second final and the nation held its collective breath. She took the first set 6-2 against another teenager, precocious Swiss talent Martina Hingis, but the wünderkind steamrollered her to take the next two and become the youngest women's champion of the century, at the age of 16. I think everyone was just relieved that Jana hadn't gone breaks up again in the second set, throwing the ball up 30 metres to serve.

TSCHÜSS

Boris was now seeded down at No.8 and even though he was only 29 it felt like he was about 49, having been around for so long. He sauntered through the tournament like an old gunslinger on a mission, until he came up against Sampras in the quarters. Mr Pistol served up a masterclass that day and the world knew what was coming when we saw a prolonged conversation between the two at the net. Boris called Pete 'the best player ever' in his press conference and promptly announced that it would be his last time on the hallowed lawns which had made his name. It was an act entirely appropriate for the brilliantly emotional boxer he always was[xxxv]. Clearly punch drunk, he followed that with the commercially incorrect, 'Unfortunately, he owns the Centre Court now, I used to own it a few years back.' Becker later expanded, 'I don't want to come back being No.60 in the world and praying that I get a good draw to win a couple of rounds. That's not my style.'[41] Sampras went on to lift another champion's trophy without breaking too much sweat, which was very much his style.

---

41 This is exactly what he did.

Ladies' Champion *Martina Hingis*
Gentlemen's Champion *Pete Sampras*

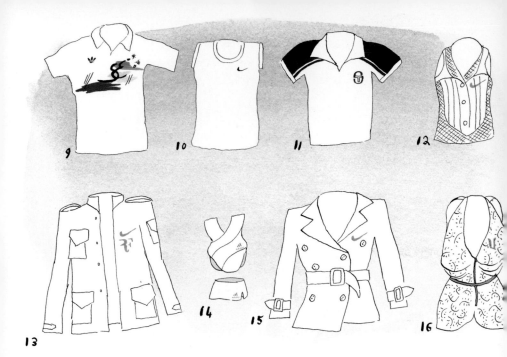

WHITE NOISE

Part 2

9. Adidas made personal shirts for their represented players and in the 80s that was largely Ivan Lendl and **Stefan Edberg**. Edberg's high point came in 1988 with a kind of Picasso-inspired paint-splattered Guedbergica 'SE' number.

10. **Rafael Nadal** was not the first person to sport the sleeveless look, but he was certainly the first to bring it to global attention in 2005. Much like ladies with lovely legs wearing hot pants, if you had biceps like that you'd skip the sleeves as well.

11. As one of the first players to sign an official endorsement, **John McEnroe** had been wearing Tacchini since the late 70s and would do until 1985, when he switched to Nike and never won another Major. This 1984 number was the high-water mark. And it's pronounced 'Tack-eeny'.

12. The **Maria Sharapova** tuxedo, a bib-fronted 2008 pinny, proved somewhat divisive in the locker room. Sharapova's Russian conqueror, Alla Kudryavtseva, said: 'I was pleased to beat her – I didn't like her outfit.'

13. Up Where He Belongs. When **Roger Federer** strode on to court dressed in a suit jacket with airline styling in 2007, he might have charmed the Home Counties, but most sane people thought he looked like he was going to a fancy dress party as An Officer and a Gentleman.

14. When asked if her dresses were getting shorter in 1998 **Anna Kournikova** replied, with a straight face, 'It's not really a shorter skirt, I just have longer legs.' It was an excellent point.

15. **Serena Williams** informed the waiting press that she loved coats, and used that as an excuse for this little belter, also from sartorial *annus mirabilis*, 2008. You can't say she got it wrong by wearing a mackintosh in preparation for the wettest Grand Slam of them all.

16. Years ahead of the fashion curve, **Venus Williams** wore a lacey onesie playsuit in 2011, and looked every bit the style trailblazer her little sis tries so hard to emulate.

SUMMER SCHOOL

Football served up a highly anticipated World Cup in France, but couldn't dovetail with the tennis as perfectly as it did in 1990. By the first Wednesday OUR HEROES were out, heroically not beating Argentina, after anti-heroic behaviour from quite-soon-to-be-heroic-again David Beckham. It was hard to keep up.

I spent an enjoyable six hours in The Queue with a wise older couple, both ex-teachers from Yorkshire, who shared tea from their Thermos, before enlightening me on the rise and fall of croquet as a modern sport. After a boom in the 1800s it had faded from popularity and was gradually sidelined at Wimbledon. The name remained in the title of the 'All England Lawn Tennis & Croquet Club', but was in itself a little misleading, as there weren't even any pitches on the main grounds anymore. I actually thought they might test me on it later in the day.

GREG THE PEG

Greg Rusedski turned up at Wimbledon amidst rumours that he had had his entire face tattooed with a Union Jack, but which sadly turned out to be untrue. He did arrive walking on crutches, playing, against medical/logical orders, then quitting overnight and promptly getting dumped by his fuming coach, former Edberg stalwart Tony Pickard, for his disobedience. Another former adviser, Brian Teacher, chimed in on a medieval tack, saying he was 'lacking in honour', before an unnamed Canadian colleague said he 'displays all the warmth of a game-show host'. It wasn't the best week for (Not) Grinnin' Greg.

KOURNI-KRAZY

~~Pin-up~~ ~~Tabloid lensman's dream~~ ~~Teen boys' screensaver~~ Tennis sensation Anna Kournikova pulled out before the start – 'KOURNIKOVER'[xxxvi] – to great disappointment from all newspaper editors, who had very much not received the memo about easing up on the knicker shots. One title went on to say that 'Sexy Anna' out of Wimbledon was leaving 'blokes broken-hearted', which seemed terribly romantic, as did the fact that she was allegedly getting marriage proposals 'BY THE BOXFUL'[xxxvii]. When Mary – 'THE BODY' – Pierce followed her out, the *Daily Mirror* posted a simple, solemn message, 'NOTICE TO ALL MEN: WIMBLEDON IS OVER'.

LEAN ON TIM

British tennis hopes in 1998 rested once again on the increasingly over-burdened shoulders of Mr Henman, who set off to try and do the impossible – beat the world's most confident sportsman, Pete Sampras, to a Wimbledon title. He kicked off in a grumpy mood, failing to see the funny side on quite some scale when a fan shouted out, 'Hurry up, Tim, we want to watch the football!' Faced with one of the least demanding fields in memory, Henman still played with great focus, threading a clean path through to the semis. There he gave his best-ever performance in a creditable four-set defeat to Sampras, who played like a character in a computer game, slamming down aces for fun. The problem wasn't so much Henman's game, which stood up well, but the crowd's lack of response to him, wildly contradicting the fervent flag-waving seen before. For a home favourite to come out in a semi-final, playing the tennis of his life, and be greeted so sombrely said a lot about overall expectation. Sampras assured him, and us, that, 'There's no doubt that Tim will come back and win this thing one day,' adding, with no hint of a grin, 'I cannot say enough good things about him.' Sampras then beat Ivanisevic in the final, who assured us of his feelings equally succinctly after his five-set defeat, 'I go kill myself.'

THE EMANCIPATION OF JANA

Once again the women picked up the excitement baton with the incredible Jana Novotna resurrection story. Five years on from her epic implosion she stood once again on the brink of the title, having seen off the increasingly chippy Martina Hingis in the semis. Simon Barnes in *The Times* talked of the 'demons of doubt' that stalked her and Tony Banks in the *Daily Express* talked about her banishing 'demons'. Basically everyone talked about these evil spirits circling above her as if she was called Regan and spent all day tied to a bed in her nightie. Novotna apparently didn't need a coach, she needed a priest.

Incredibly, she sailed through the final against Nathalie Tauziat, winning in straight sets, the relieved Duchess of Kent telling her that it was 'third time lucky', and embracing her in that warm and gracious way of hers. It was a sporting moment to cherish; 'CRY FREEDOM', 'NOGOTYA' and 'TEARS OF JOY'[xxxviii], the papers chimed as we all sobbed in living rooms across the nation.

BB, true to his word, was nowhere to be seen in a sporting sense, but then showed up in the commentary booth, looking like he had wandered in from a night out at Tramp, before delivering a first-class job for the semi-finals. Everyone was full of the fact that he didn't want payment but instead wanted to 'give back' to this place that made his name. It was classic Boris. It was actually Borisian.

YOUNG GUNS

The Boys' singles champion was a guy called Roger Federer, who I remembered for the fact that he had curtains in his hair, making him look like he was in an indie band, and that someone told me his surname meant 'trader in feathers' in old German. The Feather Trader beat Georgian Itakli Labadze 6-4, 6-4 in front of 200 or so people on No.1 Court. *The Independent* posed itself a tricky question, 'So is Federer a future Wimbledon champion? Probably not, unless he learns to vary his tactics.' Maybe he read that piece.

Ladies' Champion Jana Novotna
Gentlemen's Champion Pete Sampras

DOWN IN THE BOONDOCKS OF ROEHAMPTON

The week before the big event I made my first visit to the Wimbledon qualifying tournament in Roehampton, on the Bank of England sports club's grass courts. Three and a half miles away from the AELTC, it is where British dreamers, ageing pros looking for one last tilt and ambitious young guns turn up and battle for a place at SW19. The event is played on tightly packed courts where kids run riot with ice lollies and fans often talk loudly between points. If you can crawl your way out of the three gruelling rounds played over four days then you are through to the Big One, even though you'll probably be knackered by then. In 1977, John McEnroe was an 18-year-old with energy to spare and a point to prove when he wrestled his way through this qualifying quagmire, then a further five rounds, all the way to the semi-finals of the main event.

BB COMES BACK TO SAY GOODBYE (AGAIN)

Having retired like a boxer, Boris came back like one, primed for one final hurrah, just as he didn't predict. The swansonging legend took five sets (and saved three match points) on No.2

Court in beating Brit Miles Maclagan in the first round, milking it for all it was worth and putting his attendant, heavily pregnant, wife, Barbara, through a whole world of stress. The crowd lapped it up by the bucket-load, as Boris defied anti-climactic death on 'The Graveyard of Champions'. 'BELOVED BECKER IS AN OLD ROMANTIC', cheered the *Daily Mirror,* strangely taking the German side, and managing to not make any references to war. The crowd's love affairs at SW19 are often not so much with the underdogs as with the real 'big dogs' and Becker the giant Schnauzer was receiving more crowd support than our own player. We love the ones who 'let you in' a bit, who let you see the inner workings, and I always felt the crowd took to Becker so passionately because of this openly emotional vulnerability, allowing us to live it all with him. It was certainly true on a personal level.

HOW MANY UNION JACKS IS TOO MANY UNION JACKS?

Centre Court in 1999 was beginning to resemble 'The Last Night of The Proms', as a nationalistic fervour swirled around The Grounds, spilling out into every nook and cranny, from picnic rugs and flasks to trousers and jester hats. These jingoistic face painters cheered the opponent's faults, screamed for 'Tiger Tim' and blubbed on the hill when the inevitable came to pass.

A FULL INDIAN

I stood in line on Friday morning, taking a cab from my house in Brixton at 3.00am on my own, and waiting there for seven hours on the street next to a whole family originally from India. The Khans had come all the way down from Edgbaston on the train the night before and had brought enough food to feed the entire Queue, a task they made a decent attempt at achieving. For the uninitiated, deep fried cheese curd really hits the spot for breakfast but a Dahi kebab is quite challenging before 6am.

MICRO MELTDOWN

There was a right old furore surrounding Anna Kournikova, even before she stepped on court. The big attention-grabber was photographed in Communist Red, with matching military beret, playing a tennis racket like a phallic guitar and knowingly flashing her white pants for the cover of a (misleadingly titled) magazine, called *Total Sport*. She then strode into the tournament sporting a 'micro dress', sending the whole of Fleet Street into meltdown, as they compared the offending item (again) to the one half-worn in the fabled Athena poster, unimaginatively titled, 'Tennis Girl'. This was a gross misjudgement as the 1976 image featured a woman wearing a normal tennis dress, but with no undies. This was also a complete non-story, as most tennis dresses since just after the Suzanne Lenglen period could be considered micro-dresses – have you seen Virginia Wade's little number for the '77 final? It's positively outrageous.

The papers were having an absolute riot, one running 'KOURNA-KORNER'[xxxix] and vowing, almost threateningly, to 'RUN A PIC A DAY TIL ANNA GOES OUT (DON'T WORRY FELLAS, SHE'S IN THE DOUBLES TOO)'. Her defeat at the hands of Venus Williams in the fourth round ('FAREWELL TO THE SUNSHINE'[xl]) saw grown male journalists bashing their heads repeatedly against their desks in extreme frustration.

MARTINA, TOO

Elsewhere in the women's game the up-and-coming younger Williams sister, Serena, fresh from a win over Steffi Graf,

withdrew due to illness, leaving the spotlight to another young star, Martina Hingis. World No.1 Hingis was experiencing something of a backlash after a disastrous French Open Final defeat to Steffi[xli] and followed that up with a bizarre 6-2, 6-0 capitulation in the first round here to Jelena Dokic. Media focus turned to the new school of 'Pushy Parents', with Martina boasting a ferocious maternal one and her conqueror Dokic a vaguely homicidal paternal one. He was soon to be seen smashing up a mobile phone and getting ejected from the grounds, clutching a George Cross flag and wildly pledging his allegiance to the Queen. You couldn't make this stuff up.

TSCHÜSS! NO, REALLY...

Becker's remarkable journey continued as he brushed aside No.15 seeded countryman, Nicolas Kiefer, then future champion Lleyton Hewitt, both in straight sets. In the fourth round he hit the wall against No.2 seed Patrick Rafter, but by then it didn't matter, we were all just looking forward to more gushing obituaries. He departed once again in triumph, one of Wimbledon's greatest loves, saying that Agassi was the best player he beat at Wimbledon. His regrets included never besting Sampras, only winning three of seven finals he competed in, but most of all not playing his good friend 'Johnny Mac'. *The Guardian* noted the standing ovation he received from the Royal Box. 'At Wimbledon this is a peerage.' His countryman Franz Beckenbauer called him 'by far the greatest sportsman Germany has ever had', but the old romantic said it all best in that endearingly honest, Borisian way of his, 'This has been a great love affair.'

NO FEAR

My only-ever showcourt ticket freebie came via a friend's Dad, but left me feeling strangely underwhelmed and longing for my spiritual home with the Great Unwashed, who had braved their way through the long night just to be there.

The British No.1, Henman was playing well but unwisely started talking about his 'day of destiny', adding 'I don't fear Pete any more.' This made it seem like he had feared Pete in last year's semi-final, which I wish I had known when I'd started watching. Henman's latest semi-final played out in a similar vein, Sampras winning in four sets ... he was simply unplayable[42].

The men's final then served up the best-possible option, with a resurgent and reinvigorated Agassi facing the unplayable Pete, prompting hopes of a reignition of their continued rivalry. The dominant power game was undeniably reducing spectators' enjoyment overall and tennis really needed Agassi to win. Agassi really didn't win, leaving Sampras with an other-worldly six titles.

---

42 Henman and Sampras played a total of seven times – Henman getting his only win in their last match in 2000.

Ladies' Champion *Lindsay Davenport*
Gentlemen's Champion *Pete Sampras*

TALKING A GOOD GAME

The tournament started with the now standard procedure of Greg and Tim plastered all over the papers, forced into making grandiose (newspaper) vows such as Tim's regal 'THIS YEAR I'M READY TO REIGN' and Greg's 'I CAN WIN IT, THERE'S NO-ONE TO FEAR'[xlii], which was quite plainly not true.

A Millennium Champions' Parade for winners and repeat finalists saw Sidney Wood, the 89-year-old 1931 champion, take a bow and also Björn Borg, who had not been back since he had lost to McEnroe in the 1981 final. The ice-cool Swede knelt down and kissed the grass as he left, the most poignant moment of an emotional day.[xliii]

RETAIL IS DETAIL

Everyone in the SW19 area suddenly seemed to have cottoned on to the enormous commercial opportunity existing with the ever-growing Queue. Locals were selling straight off their driveways, like high-end car boot sales, with everything from greasy burgers to knock-off t-shirts, from plastic British bulldogs and London snowglobes to weird little pieces of tennis jewellery. I half expected to see a sparkly-eyed old lady in a shawl offering palm readings and crystal ball sessions. Local people living in castles worth millions of pounds were standing outside offering car parking at £20 a pop – it didn't add up. Or maybe it totally added up and was exactly the kind of thinking that gets you a castle worth millions of pounds in the first place.

SERIAL OFFENDER

When Violet Fane said, 'All good things come to those who wait', she was clearly not referring to The Queue on a wet Thursday. When you spend all night sleeping on a pavement it is a real kick in the nuts when you then don't get to see any tennis at all. Especially when you have been strong-armed, by physical proximity, into having a three-hour conversation about the serial killer Dr Harold Shipman with a mortgage broker from Dungeness, who seemed to have far too much knowledge on the minutiae of the case. When I asked him to stop talking about it in the most direct way, 'Can you please stop talking about Harold Shipman?', he looked upset and then informed me, for no apparent reason, that there is no word in the English language which rhymes with 'month'.

AND SHE PLAYS TENNIS!

Anna Kournikova was getting further each year from the 'thrilling tennis player who reached a semi-final' and closer to a 'celebrity who sometimes plays tennis in between more pressing engagements'. In the year 2000 other engagements included a massive advertising campaign for a new sports bra, which featured the less-than-subtle tagline 'ONLY THE BALL SHOULD BOUNCE' and a tennis party at the Palace, where she was pap'd even more than fellow guest Elizabeth

Hurley, no doubt irritating La Safety Pin enormously. She was then the victim of a relentlessy determined male streaker, described in the papers as 'unemployed', but basically a big perv who was apparently dropping his velcro pants for the 157th time. The Golden Girl hid her face in her towel and went out in the second round.

UPWARDLY MOBILE

It was the year when the whole world suddenly had a mobile phone, and every time one rang in the silence of the court the whole place fell about laughing as though Basil Fawlty had just goose-stepped across the grass. When the umpire then asked everybody to keep their phones turned off half the stadium would applaud with solemnity, as if we'd all had quite enough phone-noise fun for now. Even in The Queue people had started ordering pizzas on their phones and getting them sent out to their Queue Numbers, negotiating delivery using this new-fangled technology. I still had a lime green BT phonecard.

* SIGH *

Back on the court and the fearless British march to victory was not going to plan. Vince Spadea was an American tennis player who came into the tournament having not won a match since October 1999, a lengthy nine months. This was not due to injury, but because he had built up the worst run in modern tennis history by simply losing, all the time. It got so bad that the press nicknamed him the 'Charlie Brown of tennis', in reference to the *Peanuts* cartoon character's long-suffering bad luck and ongoing 'loser' status. You can already see where this was going.

Grinnin' Greg came in to Wimbledon as No.14 seed but was ousted by Charlie in five sets, 9-7 in the fifth. 'FLOP

RUSEDSKI BEATEN BY WORLD'S BIGGEST LOSER',
the *Daily Mirror* shouted, almost excitedly.

Heads turned to that altogether more British of
institutions, Tim Henman, who, at 25, was definitely
coming in to his prime. First round defeats in a tune-up
at Nottingham, and then at Queen's didn't bode well but,
after his splendid efforts in the last two years, hopes were
still unreasonably high. He cruised through the first rounds
but came a cropper against Mark 'The Scud' Philippoussis,
an Australian who might have been designed by Disney.
The Scud (nickname due to his exocet missile of a serve) was
ruggedly handsome and had the upper body they depict for
incredible musclemen in cartoons, bashing the High Striker
in fairgrounds. Having knocked out Rusedski in '99 he was
getting quite a taste for the British-ish blood.

BELLE OF THE BALL

Venus Williams got to her first final, mixing up the women's
game in a way it massively needed post Martina/Chrissie/
Steffi. It was her Dad who showed himself to be the real star
turn on the day, with his incredibly weird 'marker pen and
white board' routine. It was a bit like a modern take on Bob
Dylan's 'Subterranean Homesick Blues' video, in which he
holds up cards displaying the lyrics.

Gleeful Mr Williams held up his first board before the
match, with a loving message to his wife at home before
showing 'THE BRITISH FANS ARE BEST FANS IN THE
WORLD', 'I NEED AN ICE COLD COCA-COLA' and,
in victory, the rather sour-tasting 'IT'S VENUS' PARTY
AND NO-ONE'S INVITED'. 'WE LOVE YOU DUKE
AND DUCHESS' followed, as a clear attempt to get back in
favour with the fans via the Royal Box. Wimbledon had never
seen anything like it.

Like a kid at sports day watching in horror as their Dad attempts the sack race after eight bottles of lager from the refreshments tent, victorious Venus looked on nervously, replacing her natural smile with one she had stuck on.

LOOK MUM, NO HANDS ... AND THIRTEEN MAJORS!

Sampras dropped the odd set here and there (possibly out of *ennui*) and played the entirely likeable (he often shouted 'Sorry, mate' if his serve toss went awry) Australian, Pat Rafter, in the drizzly, rain-interrupted final. Sampras wrapped it up comfortably after a tight first couple of sets and claimed his record-breaking seventh title. It was impossible to ignore the size of the achievement as the American went ahead of Roy Emerson with a whopping 13 Major titles in total. Close to tears he climbed the stands, in the now semi-traditional way, to embrace his parents, who were incredibly attending for the first time. Jeez, what does a kid have to do to get a little parental approval?

Ladies' Champion *Venus Williams*
Gentlemen's Champion *Pete Sampras*

THE DAILY SMASH
Classic Wimbledon Headlines

The newspapers' significance to my Wimbledon experience over the years could really not be overstated. I very much agree with Chief Justice Earl Warren, who said, 'I always turn to the sports pages first, which record people's accomplishments. The front page has nothing but man's failures.' Here are some particular favourites from some long mornings on the pavement.

ANYONE FOR ENNIS?
The *Daily Mirror* moves on from Murray's 2012 final defeat with Olympic spirit.

WINNING'S UPSET MY LOVE MATCH
TODAY reports how Jeremy Bates got his priorities right when he booked his stag do for the second week of Wimbledon '92. Or wrong. Depending on your priorities.

FAMILY POWER STRUGGLE WON BY THE SERENER WILLIAMS
The *Daily Telegraph* get it spot on in 2000.

RUN OVER BY A LORI
The Sun deal Steffi Graf some shock treatment in '92 after she crashed out to Lori McNeil.

LAST TARANGO IN SW19
Jeff fumes his way off court, leaving the floor to his emotive French wife, who finished the job with aplomb. Thankfully no mention of butter in *The Observer*.

THEY THINK IT'S KOURNIKOVA ... IT IS NOW
In '98 Anna Kournikova was ripe for a pun or two, even if they made no sense. Quite what Kournikova had to do with commentary from the 1966 World Cup Final, you'd have to ask *The Sun*.

HAIL KING BORIS OF ENGLAND
When Boris came back (to say goodbye) in '99, the *Daily Mirror* claimed him as our own.

WILD THING V MILD THING
In 2001 the country's hopes were high, as even-keeled Tim faced completely-off-his-rocker Goran and the *Daily Mirror* stirred it up.

with apologies to EH Shepard

HOT AND BOTHERED

The ascendant internet made everything seem to spin faster in 2001, with MPs thumping members of the public, the launch of the iPod, royal butlers acting up and something called 'Beckhamania' becoming a genuine mania, unlike the Hen one. SW19 experienced temperatures in the mid-90s, the Wimbledon shop promptly sold out of sunblock and a ball girl collapsed on court. No.1 seed Martina Hingis staged the sporting equivalent, as once again she got dumped out emphatically in the first round, once again by an unseeded player.

In other news David Lloyd suggested that Wimbledon's grass was providing 'unwatchable' tennis, adding that they should replace it with synthetic carpet, which could 'still be green'. This fact was hard to argue with, as it would undeniably still be green, even if 'being green' was not the prerequisite for a successful tennis court playing surface.

In truth he had a point about the tennis, which had become painfully monotonous on the men's side. There were rumours that the Club had started to use a different grass, a denser soil and a softer, heavier ball to counter the power generated with the new technologies and bring some finesse back to the grass court game. Another rumour, that Pete Sampras was going to be asked to play with one hand tied behind his back, proved to be wide of the mark.

IVAN THE REALLY RATHER TERRIBLE
It had been a controversial year for wildcards, with loads dished out to wildly unsuccessful Brits, on a seemingly endless wild cycle. Goran Ivanisevic had also been given one, what with him being the kind of tennis star Wimbledon fans grow to love – the plucky loser, the thrice losing finalist nearly man, who we used to love to hate and now kind of love to love. At No.128 in the world Goran said, 'If this is my last year, I haven't hurt my pride. At the end of the year I will have a long and interesting conversation with myself and see what me and me decide.' He would tell anyone who would listen that he was playing tennis 'because I don't have anything else to do ... I'm playing like an idiot, just serve and forehand and then I miss'. Barely winning any matches all year, he had recently suffered the ignominy of losing to one Hyung-Taik Lee in Brighton, when he was disqualified after running out of rackets, having smashed up the three he brought along.

AS HAPPY AS BARRY
World No.265 Barry Cowan beat another Brit to set up a decidedly long shot at seven-time champion Pete Sampras. The papers were full of the fact that Barry lived with his parents and travelled around in a Ford Fiesta whereas Sampras travelled in a private jet and probably didn't live with his parents. Especially as they could so rarely be arsed to watch him play. But Barry had a secret weapon – his personal stereo. The Liverpool fan was repeatedly listening to the inspirational Mersey tune, 'You'll Never Walk Alone',

and so far it was working a treat. Unbelievably he walked through the storm of going two sets down, held his head high by clawing it back to level terms and the hope in his heart nearly caused an upset on a titanic scale, before the champ edged it.

Promising UK youngster, Jamie Delgado, who was once unofficially the world's best teen when he won the Orange Bowl in Miami, but was now ranked at No.182, followed his lead, and he didn't even need Gerry & The Pacemakers. Delgado beat Medvedev, now coached by Wimbledon pantomime villain Jeffrey 'Jeff' Tarango, who, in no way being ironic, but certainly offensive, said <u>afterwards</u> that Delgado was 'only good enough to beat retards'. Delgado crashed out to Agassi in the next round and by Friday all the Queen's ladies and all the Queen's men, bar Greg and Tim, were gone. This made it the perfect timing for the diplomatic sports minister, Richard Caborn, to make a visit to the tournament and say, 'I'm not keen on tennis. I'm not staying to watch any matches.'

SHE AIN'T HALF HOT, MUM

The papers were tiring of Kournikova's lack of presence on the actual court and turned their attention instead to Barbara 'Babsi' Schett from Austria and Lina Krasnoroutskaya, the virtually unpronounceable rising star from Russia. The brilliantly named Israeli player, 'Anna Smashnova', would have been a much better bet for tabloid limelight, but she went out in the first round. Babsi helped herself no end when she agreed to a sponsorship deal with the *Daily Mirror*, announcing after her first win, 'I hope Mirror readers are proud of me. I did it for them.' One watching 16-year-old lad was interviewed and sighed, 'She is lovely to look at.' His pimply friend, gleefully rubbing his palms up and down his thighs, added, 'I'd love to give her my mobile number', implying that the lack of digit knowledge was all that was stopping gorgeous 25-year-old multi-millionairess Babsi from getting in touch.

COMMUNITY SPIRIT

The *Daily Telegraph* referred to The Queue as 'one of London's most transient communities', which suggested that people were actually living there. I totally skipped the transients and eschewed the sleeping out part as my early tournament presence was limited to two evenings after work. Despite its passive appeal to the armchair fan, it was surprisingly difficult to persuade anyone to come and stand in a line with me for the best part of four hours to watch a set and a half of Voltchkov against Doseděl. On my second visit I waited for over three hours, sandwiched between a family of four from Seoul, who could not speak a single word of English but were so charming that they were just nice to be around, and a group of German teen boys who thought farting 'at' each other was the height of hilarity.

SWISS ON A ROLL

Pete Sampras was looking a far cry from the legend he had become but the world was still shocked by his defeat to a Swiss guy more famous for his Christopher Robin-style bobbed haircut and fractured 'hairline temperament'. Roger Federer, the former Boys' champ, informed the world, 'I'm a winner since I cut out the tantrums', and promptly made Pete look very much like he belonged in a different era[43]. In the next round Federer strangely found Our Tim too hot to handle and the nation roared in support.

---

43 It would be the only time the two would ever play competitively.

FEE, FI, FO, FUM, I SMELL THE BLOOD OF AN ENGLISHMAN

Hammier than a ham sandwich, Greg Rusedski had come in to the fourth round battle with Goran Ivanisevic boasting an eight-match losing run against 'The Divided One', who was really justifying his wildcard and starting to play a bit. Famously self-analytical Goran revealed, 'In every game I play there are three players in me that could surface anytime; Good Goran, Bad Goran, Crazy Goran! They can all serve aces.' He then stoked the fires by implying that Rusedski was a bottler and promptly smashed him in straight sets, confirming that his split personality issues were in check, explaining that both principal sides were 'good friends now, they are both thinking the same way and they're both in London.' 'Two Gorans too many for Rusedski', the *Daily Telegraph* wryly observed.

TIM'S TOMORROW

Tim Henman's defining match at Wimbledon, unfortunately for him, was played against all of the Gorans. This one, Henman's third semi-final, was arguably the most winnable, against an emotionally fractured Ivanisevic supposedly struggling with a shoulder injury. Rain stopped play overnight and *The Sun* led with, 'IT'S RAINING HEN!', referencing a very camp disco song about each and every woman being able to find their perfect guy, for absolutely no reason. In reality, Henman was almost over the line with a solid lead, Bad Goran having played the entire second set in 14 minutes, winning only four points, and getting himself in a right tizz. The next slice of action in the rain-destroyed match saw Goran get back in the groove and the third installment saw him steal it in a fifth set of extreme tension, played on the Sunday afternoon Gentlemen's final slot. Oh the irony. Timothy would not be the first man since 1938 to match Bunny's feat of reaching the final. Now there's a phrase you'll only hear in tennis.

Goran would return the next day for 'The People's Monday' – a final for the fans, pitting him against laid-back Aussie, Pat Rafter. Unfortunately I had a morning meeting booked at the Mars factory in Slough, at which we were discussing whether to add a new character to the fictional Milky Way Magic Stars gang.

WIMBLEFEST
By the time they announced it would be a complete free-for-all on the ticket front I knew that I was in last chance saloon at my job; with no holiday to take, a day already bunked off the week before and a boss who had my number. So I did the smart thing. I headed straight up to Church Road with Bally on Sunday night, planning to take yet another sickie.

The carnival atmosphere outside on the street was more akin to a football crowd, with bonfires, barbecues, singalongs, fireworks and a noticeable absence of tents, as most seemed resolved to the idea of not sleeping much. The group of four lads next to us from Adelaide displayed this attitude by bringing 96 cans of lager between them. They were also remarkable for the fact that three of them were called 'Brett'.

The crowd were split roughly in half, in a way that tennis only experiences at the Davis Cup, creating a decidedly surreal air around The Queue. I barely slept, feeling decidedly jangly, and by 9am I was checking my new mobile phone every five seconds, dreading a text or call from work to check on my health. Ten minutes later my worst fear was confirmed with a message so curt from my boss that it made me physically shudder. An hour later I was at my desk in Great Portland Street, as Bally tucked into his seventh can of Foster's.

THE WILDEST CARD

The Rafter v Ivanisevic match unfolded in a thrilling way, an endless stream of breakneck serve and volley tennis for a raucous throng, greeting every point as if it was a last-minute winner in a cup final. The match was so emotional that it seemed in no way out of the ordinary when Ivanisevic openly prayed on match point at 8-7 in the fifth. The cartoon giant closed it out and the embrace at the end was as warm as I had ever seen. Goran, the only wildcard ever to win a Major, came up with one of the great Wimbledon quotes when, bleary-eyed, he said: 'If I never win another match I don't care. Whatever I do in my life, wherever I go, I'm going to always be a Wimbledon champion.' I heard afterwards that Pat Rafter had walked up to the Dog & Fox pub in Wimbledon village that evening and bought 'the house' a round. I don't know if this is true or not, but some anecdotes are best left unchecked.

Ladies' Champion *Venus Williams*
Gentlemen's Champion *Goran Ivanisevic*

ONE FOOT TOO FEW

Most of England was praying that Beckham's broken foot held up for the most overhyped World Cup in history, in Japan and Korea, the patched-up hero hobbling around the Land Of The Rising Sun on one leg like Greg. It didn't, but he did sell three billion replica shirts and lead the team to glorious victory defeat against Brazil, just the way we like it – wronged, this time by a keeper with a dodgy ponytail. Getting sacked by an ad agency only had a beneficial effect on my queuing as by early June I was out of work, and raring to go. The Queue rightly returned to that special place in my heart. I had a lot of place to fill.

I DON'T WANT TO BELIEVE

On the Wednesday I met one of the strangest characters I had ever encountered in my life, and by far the strangest in The Queue. I am slightly scared of naming him, so let's call him 'Naughty Raymond'. He was one of those very understated posh chaps who, wearing his grandfather's (probably very expensive) shabby jumper, might have stepped out of the pages of a Mary Wesley novel about wealthy country folk up to mischief in the Cotswolds. It started off innocently enough, with an anecdote about how, in HG Wells' *The War Of The Worlds*, the sixth Martian invasion cylinder landed in Wimbledon. It became clear that he was obsessed by time travelling and soon had me involved in a very unsettling conversation about whether we were actually there, in The Queue, that day at all. His eerily lucid and enticing voice then started talking about concepts of derealisation, disassociation from the external world, the State of the Dead and even a movement he terrifyingly referred to as 'The New International'. It led to not just the worst night's sleep I had ever had in The Queue, but one of the worst night's sleep I had ever had in general.

NEVER CONFUSE CHARISMA WITH A LOUD VOICE

Naughty Raymond was proof that you meet an incredible breadth of characters in The Queue, and some of them are a lot more interesting than others. Naughty was an example of a compelling, if petrifying, one. But there's a big difference between a character, in the sense of an individual or human whose characteristics are the aggregate of their features and traits, often referred to affectionately, and someone who thinks of themselves as 'A Character'. With a capital C, often an unpalatable person. One of those types whose exaggerated personality traits have been sharpened to the point of being painful to other humans. These self-consciously eccentric weirdos occur in about 0.0001 per cent of normal life, but about 15 per cent of Queue life – standing still in a line for 24-plus hours to watch tennis just tends to attract this type of person.

On Thursday I had the misfortune to come across someone from this latter, Capital Camp. They are almost always male, the female form is probably 'kooky', a mildly irritating, but considerably less bothersome stereotype. The zany guy was wearing one of those caps which enables the wearer to carry a can of drink on each side of their head, making them look like Mickey Mouse, and drink from them both at once, like a great big funster. Why anyone would need to do this is beyond most people's wildest imaginations but in this case, as if the humour of the double can was just too darn obvious, he had replaced drinks with apples. This ignored the fact that you can't drink from an apple with anything, let alone a cheap plastic straw, but it did get him some attention. And that's what they love, A Character, attention.

FAR FROM THE MADDING CROWD

'I'VE GOT THE POWER … I reckon I can Go ALL The Way'[xliv], Greg said in the paper, and 'ONE DAY I'LL BE CHAMPION', Tim confidently informed us in another[xlv]. The Brits then spluttered into action, Greg saying, 'I'm gonna get better – it's my new target', which was reassuring, but

made you wonder what his old target was. Then he lost in the fourth round. The delirious, almost maniacal, fans just kept shrieking louder and louder, their raging faces covered in red, white and blue warpaint. *The Daily Mail* cheekily wondered if Henmania was actually 'destroying Wimbledon', questioning the 'puerile yelling, cheering and jeering'. The baying hordes contrasted with the mild-mannered Tim, who impressively reached another semi but was less impressive in being brushed aside by fellow mini-fist-pump fan Lleyton Hewitt, or 'THE EXTIMINATOR', as *The Sun* labelled him. Hewitt looked like he was over in London on a year out from Australia, spending his spare time working in a bar and having barbecues on Clapham Common, but went on to crush argy-bargy Argentinian David Nalbandian in the final. Elsewhere the Williams sisters contested the first one-family final since 1884, this time younger Serena eclipsing big sis, Venus.

LOADED QUESTIONS

Anna Kournikova, sporting a very unsettling grin/grimace, lost her playful sheen when being interviewed by the BBC's Garry Richardson, after another first round exit. The probing interviewer asked her if her confidence was low, to which she took wild offence, advising him not to 'phrase the question that way', having recently completed her masters in 'Sporting Interview Techniques for Television' from Harvard University. It seemed a fair, if provocative, question but when he then mischievously 'wondered' whether she should step down a level to play some other tournaments and rebuild her confidence she just got up to leave. The doomed discussion laboured on for a few more minutes before she said that she would 'practise and play doubles' to improve, chipping off and then getting caught playing mixed tongue doubles with Enrique Iglesias in a London nightclub.

ONE YEAR'S SEEDS MAKE THIS YEAR'S WEEDS

A year after Roger Federer had sent down 25 aces in knocking out Pete Sampras, he served just one in crashing out to teenager Mario Ančić in straight sets in the first round[44]. And that was just the beginning. 'TIMBER!' the papers cried as the big names started falling, with Safin, Agassi and then even Sampras crashing out.

Pistol stamped his foot after being asked to play world No.145 George Bastl out on the No.2 court 'graveyard' in the second round and then behaved bizarrely from the get-go. It was brilliant when they used to mix it up by putting the top players on courts outside of Centre and No.1 – it's a tradition they really should return to.

Courtside photographers zoomed in on the letter Sampras kept reading in breaks, which turned out to be a tender tome from his wife, Bridgette. It opened factually, some might say matter-of-factually, with, 'To my husband, 7-time Wimbledon champion, Pete...', before reminding him that he was 'the greatest player ever to pick up a racket', which served to make me wonder if there was a better player, but he or she had just not got round to getting the equipment. Peter took it all in, lost, shrugged those trademark shoulders and said, 'I'm not as intimidating as I once was.'

He was not in fact the only American of his generation to like a little courtside reading, as a few years earlier Jim Courier had raised eyebrows when he started to read a novel during changeovers, on his way to a defeat. Perhaps it was the book that threw him off, as *Maybe the Moon*, by Armistead Maupin, is the story of a female Jewish dwarf.

---

44 Ančić would go on to become that rarest of things; a glamorous international tennis star who quit the game to fulfil his lifelong dream of being an investment banker.

WHEN PUSHING IN COMES TO SHOVE

Like the Mods and Rockers on the south coast in 1964, I was there the night The Queue split into two warring factions, as some rowdy South Africans (already well represented in Southfields) muscled in and caused a semi-riot in SW19. Pushing in was actually quite rare, and normally a debate that us Brits will avoid having for as long as we can. Much like, 'Can you move down the carriage please?', used on a packed train or tube, the phrase, 'Did you know there is a queue?' is a tricky one. The enquirer knows full well they can move down, and similarly clearly did know that the interloper knew there was a queue, but it's nigh-on impossible to say without sounding like a hector.

The terrifying mixture of middle-aged women and students, armed only with numbered Queue cards, but charged up by gallons of Pimms, took on the Queue-jumping arriviste foreign army that evening, who had taken up an advanced position in Church Road. The combative Saffers were hurling unveiled insults and occasionally throwing in the second rudest swear word of them all, before the minor fracas was swiftly resolved by the Honorary Stewards, who we really should send in to sort out all such international quarrels. The man next to me asked the (rather perfunctory) HS if the Queue jumpers had been removed and was told sharply that, 'There was no Queue jumping.'[45] Much like the ravens and the tower, if The Championships ever do away with the Honorary Stewards, the grassy kingdom will most definitely fall.

---

45 This reminded me of that (most likely apocryphal, but still good) tale about a man's Rolls-Royce breaking down in Spain and them having to fly two engineers out to fix it. After three months without a bill he called up to enquire and was told emphatically that, 'The Rolls-Royce does not break down.'

Ladies' Champion *Serena Williams*
Gentlemen's Champion *Lleyton Hewitt*

EXCUSE MY FRENCH

The Duke of Kent, in his guise as Club President, brought in the abolition of bowing to the Royal Box, except when the 'Queen is in attendance', so effectively a complete abolition, as Elizabeth is far from being a tennis nut. My own queuing saw me spend the night between a rock and a hard place. The rock was a spacey guy called Roy who told me the almost real-time narratives of a number of his recent dreams. The nadir was reached when he told me about one in which he was a star singer of a supergroup playing a gig at Wembley stadium; Paul McCartney was on bass, Slash on lead guitar, Elton John on piano and Sue Barker on drums. The hard place on the other side was a Parisian family with two teenage children, who were so unbelievably scrappy that at one point I asked a Steward to come and check their tent as I genuinely thought the mother had killed the daughter. The young teenage daughter was clearly a handful – I could tell from the fact that she was wearing a t-shirt emblazoned with the slogan 'POURQUOI PAS?' My insomnia caused by their bickering allowed me to develop a theory that the French are essentially very similar to children:

175

- *They say hello to everyone, especially people they don't know*
- *They get in a massive mood if they think that you are not taking them seriously*
- *They speak a different language to everyone else in the world*
- *They treat pancakes as if they are a real food*
- *They forget rows and disagreements almost immediately after starting them*
- *They can totally not handle it if you tell them what to do*
- *They often go to the toilet not in a bathroom or designated toilet*
- *They can also be quite endearing*

RULE F*!*IN' BRITANNIA, YOU FR*!GIN' WA**ERS

While British tennis couldn't stop talking about a teenager called Andrew[46], every single one of our women crashed out in the first round, leading to a spate of vociferous, and perennial, criticism. *The Guardian* hopefully mocked up a photo of Tim Henman lifting the singles trophy, which wildly fate-fearing sportsmen always love, and asked various celebs if they thought it would be 'his year'. Legendarily fearless warrior 'It-Girl', Lady Victoria Hervey, said: 'I just don't know if he has the courage to do it.'

Elsewhere, the mood of rage continued on Centre Court where, two sets down to big-serving American Andy Roddick, a Non-Grinnin' Greg Rusedski was still up 5-2 in the third, and very much in the match. An A-Rod forehand landed on the baseline, 'Out!' came the call (from a spectator) and Greg duly stopped playing. The umpire refused to play a let and Rusedski was riled, promptly losing his serve before launching into a tirade at the umpire of which Johnny Mac would have

---

46 More on him later.

been ~~proud~~ ashamed. 'I can't do anything if the crowd f**king calls it,' he raged. 'Absolutely f**king ridiculous. At least replay the point.' 'Obscenities were spewing out of Rusedski's mouth like a soiled fountain,' *The Guardian* observed, as Greg displayed his full, and impressively broad, repertoire of British swearwords. To think they doubted his allegiances. 'F**king ridiculous, frigging ridiculous. Some wa**er in the crowd changes the whole match and you allow it to happen. Well done … Absolutely shit.' He proved his point further by losing every remaining game, and out he went.

The Sun managed to track down 'The Lout Who Shouted Out', 29-year-old Lithuanian Evaldas Ziolinis, who appeared sheepishly (ill-advisedly wearing a Man Utd shirt) and blubbed that he was, 'Absolutely gutted. I want to apologise to Greg and to British tennis fans', and offered to pay the £1,500 Rusedski was fined for the outburst. He also revealed that his girlfriend was 'hardly speaking to him' and swore that he would never set foot in Wimbledon again. Scant reward for Greg. Henman, to the sound of a giant clock ticking in his

28-year-old ears, went one round further but lost to middling Frenchman Sebastien Grosjean in the quarters.

SHORT SHRIFT

2003 was the year Robby Ginepri proudly became the first man to wear a sleeveless shirt in SW19, but the pressure of sartorial trailblazing all got too much and he went out in the first round. His fellow American Ashley Harkleroad wore a similarly minimal item – a teeny weeny skirt which she twinned with even weenier white lycra shorts. 'BOT A DISGRACE', the *Daily Express* shrieked, rubbing its hands with glee[47]. There were new young gunslingers all around but Lleyton Hewitt, No.1 seed and defending champion, crashed out in the first round to the giant Croatian world No.203 Ivo Karlovic.

Rafa Nadal, a man-child with a surname that means 'Christmas' in Catalan, became the youngest 17-year-old since BB to reach the third round and also managed to extend the overall length of (already long) men's shorts by about 25cm. In the 80s men's shorts were effectively hot pants, Daisy Dukes for the sporting arena, as worn by WHAM! with great pride. And the addition of shuttlecocks. This was an era when McEnroe was keeping the hemlines high and the material-loathing Becker and Lendl were more than willing to follow. It was only the arrival of Agassi and Sampras in the early 90s that changed it all, following basketball and football's leads with their outrageously lengthy Bermudas. Ten years on and Rafa's new surfy board shorts, when socks were pulled up, were so long that they left just a tantalising five centimetres of bare flesh on the upper shin.

---

47 She'd wear even less a few years later when becoming the first tennis player to appear in *Playboy*.

ROGER, ROGER

Roger Federer, or the 'Feder Duster', as he was nicknamed by *The Sun*, for his deftness of touch with the racket, had thrown off the shackles of his temper tantrum past and started to embrace his own considerable talent with gusto. After his breakthrough beating Pistollero he had been slow to live up to his 'next big thing' tag, often losing early in the Majors. In these two weeks he dropped just one set, winning his first Major and also joining an elite group to have won both the Boys' and the Men's titles at Wimbledon[48]. He did it playing a new-but-old-look brand of balletic, almost Laver-ian, tennis zoned in from some kind of Zen planet. Talking of other planets, Boris was beamed in to comment on Roger, then stared off into the middle distance, as if tuning in to telecommunications from another galaxy, somewhat cosmically pronouncing, 'The future has come today.'

THE PAST IS PRESENT

In other finals Martina won her 20th title, the mixed doubles, at the tender age of 46, matching her chum, Billie Jean King. Potential heir to the iconic throne, Serena Williams, defended the giant plate, once again beating big sis in the final, as the two of them destroyed the rest of the field with incredible superheroine powers and the most disruptive attire we'd seen since Lenglen.

---

48 Björn Borg, Pat Cash and Stefan Edberg were the others.

Ladies' Champion *Serena Williams*
Gentlemen's Champion *Roger Federer*

THE UNIVERSITY OF (QUEUE) LIFE

Now that Wimbledon has moved back a week in the calendar the significance of the higher education graduate has increased considerably. As they have now all finished their taxing studies they can all get in The Queue from the off – leading to the heaving numbers now seen in the first week.

They are often in exceptionally high spirits, frequently over-excited by the incredible feats of learning they have recently accomplished. They are always at Wimbledon to let off some serious steam and have a <u>massive laugh</u>. Like it or not, that's what they are going to do ...

- Being a young and innocent bunch who have been closeted away in libraries for years they are blissfully unaware of the power of their own bodies, so will manage to take out four tents, three picnics and six Japanese couples with their playful game of touch rugby, which is enjoyed by precisely zero other people. This is proven by the fact that most other Queuers stay in their tents for two hours in spite of the 96°F heat outside.

- Having lived in a scholarly bubble they have yet to re-tune their ears to acceptable volumes so they will shout a lot, very loudly. And play music from the 1980s in an ironic way, despite the fact that they were born in the mid-1990s. Again, very loudly.

- There will be some tears around 8pm, as the alcoholic comedown kicks in and we learn that they are only here because they didn't get Glastonbury tickets and in fact all their cool friends are off taking mind-bending hallucinogenics and kissing each other in a field in Somerset.

- Around 10.30pm, half the group sneak off to a nightclub in Hackney, banging on your tent to ask you if you can cover for them if an Honorary Steward comes by. Everyone knows that the HSs are always one step ahead of this sneaky game, as they have made notes of who is where and how many they are. The ill-fated sojourn to a club is doomed from the start. But plough on the Graduates will.

- At 6am, when you are awoken by the Steward, you will notice that the Graduates' Union Jack tents next door have been collapsed, and barely anything remains apart from a broken stereo and a collection of Scrumpy Jack and Pringles cans. Where once was such frivolity and abandon, this hive of fun and boundless joy is now just a crumpled mess, where a couple of the last remaining team sit clinging to each other in their retro 1980s underwear.

- In the distance are two or three more, walking gingerly along accompanied by two Honorary Stewards, wearing fluorescent face paint and sobbing quietly as the day breaks over a Centre Court they will never see.

EVERYBODY'S TALKING

One-man news outlet, John McEnroe, having recently suggested the return of wooden rackets and moving the service line closer to the net, announced that he would win playing both Williams sisters at the same time, which was in part a response to Serena's alleged comment that she fancied playing in a few men's tournaments. The one man who saw the dollar signs in putting it on was the billionaire TV laughing stock Donald Trump. As if anyone would ever take him seriously!

Boris released his autobiography, called, obviously, *The Player*, which was written entirely in the Borisian dialect and included the following line about a trip to an Elton John concert in New York: 'The atmosphere is somewhere between a carnival and a kindergarten. Outside in the car park, even the cars begin to rock to the rhythm.'[xlvi] Not everyone is fluent in Borisian.

GREEN SCREEN

The much-hyped *Wimbledon* movie was released, rather strangely, in September, just as the tennis season was winding down. It told the fictional story of Peter Colt, a privileged former star English tennis player now in the twilight of his career, who is having a tilt at one last Wimbledon. He then falls in love with an American tennis starlet with a stereotypical pushy parent, who shows him how to win, or love, or something, again. Serena Williams drily observed: 'It must be a comedy if a British player is winning at Wimbledon.'

Paul Bettany played the plucky Brit, in a role originally earmarked for Hugh Grant, which was a strange choice as Bettany looked like he was Dutch. Still, he did a good line in those Grant specialities when you say something out loud and then reprimand yourself for externalising it ... 'Oh drat, I can't believe I just said that out loud, what a wally I am. Silly sausage. Bollocks.' He had been trained for the role by Pat Cash and had mastered the art of playing tennis without a ball against a blue screen. If only it were that simple. The production arm, Working Title, had previously made *Four Weddings & A Funeral,* another film which made everyone think that all Londoners live in Belgravia, have lavish dinner parties every night and don't work much. It was met with almost complete indifference at the box office.

TEENAGE KICKS

Hot on the heels of the Kournikova ballistic missile, Russia launched another blonde testosterone rocket targeted at this corner of south-west London, in the form of the glacial Maria Sharapova. When the first, admittedly eye-catching, image of the leggy Maria being eyed up by the whole team of lustful teen boy court coverers appeared, her celebrity was assured. Proud 17-year-old Maria emphatically stated, 'I am not a bit like Anna ... I win tournaments.' Ouch. I bet Garry Richardson was laughing his head off, from his commentary

booth at a Challenger tournament in Uzbekistan. Sharapova proved her point by going on to win the whole blinking thing, beating double champ (and a slightly sulky) Serena in the final.

NUTHIN' BUT A NUMBER

Martina Navratilova caused a stir when she was given a wildcard for the singles, especially after she had received one at the previous month's French Open and duly got hammered by Gisele Dulko. The 47-year-old needed just 47 minutes, and lost only one game, to win her first round match, but was drawn to face Dulko again, this time going down in a respectable three sets. Point made.

WAR PAINT

I have always lived by the simple rule that any adult who indulges too readily in the use of face paint is an absolute stinker. This would prove useful in these patriotic times, as The Queue was getting more zealous by the year, now a virtual river of red, white and blue gushing down Church

Road. I queued quietly on my own one evening when I was interrogated on a variety of patriotic subjects by the combined force of two blokes who, when not painting each other's faces, were credit controllers from Kent. I explained that I was there to try and get in to see Goran's likely farewell, but they seemed genuinely offended that I wasn't spending the night sleeping on mud and pavement just to go and join them all day watching Henman on a giant outdoor TV screen, wearing make-up. 'Misery guts', one of the painted pair muttered as they walked off, as if my lack of face paint was making me unhappy, which it certainly wasn't.

Bad weather in 2004 led to another Middle Sunday, by which time Greg was already out, but the baying crowd of largely middle-aged Sauvignon Blanc-pumped women from Weybridge belted out 'C'mon England' at anyone whose name did not end in –ova, or –ic. Just like those louts at the football. In spite of *Debrett's* clearly instructing that 'Cheering and whooping should be kept to a minimum', they continued undeterred.

No.5 seed Henman was looking well in the mood this year, jokingly saying, 'When I'm chairman of the All England Club I'll bring in a Middle Sunday,' not at all joking. To prove it he beat The Scud and was a big HERO, but then he lost to Mario Ančić in the quarters and he was 'DIMBO', who let the nation down.

CLOSE YOUR EYES AND THINK OF SCOTLAND

'Andrew' Murray beat qualifier Myktyta Kryvonos in the Boys' event and probably didn't say, 'I want to be next hero', as quoted in the *Daily Express*, what with the obvious lack of definite article. After going out in the third round he was wisely described only as a 'promising Scottish teenager', whilst another talented Brit, Miles Kasiri, actually got to the final, where he narrowly lost out to French teen, and future star, Gaël Monfils[49].

A FEDER IN HIS CAP

Roger Federer had started to look a bit special and the defence of his title was another masterclass in which the Swiss was anything but neutral. It was not exactly a gilded age of men's tennis but 'COOL HAND ROGER', as one paper[xlvii] called him (despite the word 'Roger' in no way rhyming with 'Luke', and him never successfully eating 50 hard-boiled eggs to prove his coolness), was starting to look like he might have the mythical 'magic dust'. Grandiose statement-addict John McEnroe went further and said, 'He could be the most talented player I have ever seen,' before collapsing to the floor of the commentary booth, exhausted by his own bluster.

---

49 Injury would take care of Kasiri's bright career and he would eventually end up being suspended by the LTA for a perceived lack of effort.

Ladies' Champion *Maria Sharapova*
Gentlemen's Champion *Roger Federer*

THE ALL ENGLAND LAWN TENNIS & QUEUING CLUB

The year started well when I won a pub quiz for my team based on knowing the name of Boris Becker's conqueror in the 1987 Wimbledon second round. I was so ~~wasted~~ excited when I correctly named 'Peter Doohan' that the rest of the evening became something of a blur and the following morning I discovered that I had been googling 'Peter Doohan's phone number' at 4am. It was a lucky escape for Peter.

I found my place in The Queue dropping faster than Greg Rusedski's world ranking, as interest in the future of British tennis rose dramatically, along with the crowd numbers.

The *Daily Mail* reported on the characters you would always see at the very front of the line, including one lady called 'Mad Sue'[50], who had apparently been a fixture for more than 40 years and was a 'third generation Queuer'. It made her sound almost aristocratic.

I love a queue, (or just 'The Queue'), as much as the next person but I was beginning to think that some of these early

---

50 I have no idea who made that name up, or why. I hope it's a joke and not a barb.

arrivers might be the same folk who slept in tents for three days outside the Apple store when they brought out a new phone charger.

Down in my comfort zone in the 200s I was next to another 'Mad', this time in the shape of a *Mad Max*-alike, a non-vocal, soap-dodging Australian man wearing black leather trousers and a matching jacket, covered in buckles and fasteners. Like the drifting loner walking across the apocalyptic wasteland this introspective chap paced silently up and down Church Road, between the burger van and the portaloos, pausing only to check his military-grade canvas tarpaulin and shake his shoulder length mop of curly hair out, like he didn't know everyone was watching. The Queue seemed to be morphing into an entirely different Wimbledon experience, a bit like the Off-Broadway version of the main event and almost completely separate from the actual tennis.

A SPANIARD IN THE WORKS[xlviii]

The late Henman-Greg era was still pulling in the crowds as the ageing Brits looked worriedly over their shoulders

at the raft of young-uns coming through. Fresh from his astonishing win in the French Open Final, 19-year-old Rafael Nadal sailed in to SW19 on his pirata ship to try and send Captain Roger to Davy Jones' locker. In a wave of publicity, he was likened to a pirate due to his playing attire of long shorts/ cut-offs, bandana, sleeveless shirt and black eye patch[51]. To me he looked more like a cross between Mowgli from *The Jungle Book* and a Teenage Mutant Ninja Turtle. Playing out of an academy in Barcelona, Nadal's sometime hitting partner, upcoming Brit Andrew Murray, was also making waves after shunning the LTA and going on to win the US Open Boys' title in 2004.

SOUND BARRIER

The *Daily Mail* was having a vintage year of tennis-related nonsense, which kicked off when they dug out the dusty old Gruntometer to record Sharapova at a whopping 100 decibels, similar to a 'small aircraft'. For the sake of comparison a (non-specific) rock band came in at 80 decibels and a Harley Davidson at 85. *The Sun* picked up its competitor's mantle with a 101-decibel recording of Maria, which they likened to Joe Dolce's 1981 hit, 'Shaddap You Face', for no apparent reason.

SHIVER-ME TIM-BERS

Tim was in a spin from early on when the papers dug out his ball girl nemesis, Caroline Hall[xlix]. Ms Hall, who we were reminded was 'nearly killed' by Henman, confirmed, 'I had my 15 minutes of fame and I loved it,' adding that she couldn't even go in to McDonald's at the time of the near-decapitation, 'for fear of being recognised'. She also told how she had bumped in to Tim in the street, but he was 'in a hurry'. I bet he was. After surviving a trademark five-setter

---

51 One of these is made up.

in the first round he went down in the second in another one after imploring the crowd, not unreasonably, to 'make some f***ing noise', like a potty-mouthed stadium announcer. He then reminded them that it was 'f***in' Wimbledon' before practically biting the head off a ball boy for not getting him his Coca-Cola. Luckily Ms Hall wasn't still around.

A RIGHT SONG AND DANCE

Venus and Serena Williams became the first tennis players to be featured in a hip hop song when Snoop Doggy Dogg released 'Signs', featuring Justin Timberlake. The cheery little ditty included the line, 'You'll see Venus and Serena, in the Wimbledon … Arena.' Only someone with the street credibility of Snoop could rename Centre Court the 'Wimbledon Arena', but it inspired Venus sufficiently to lift the trophy again. It wasn't even the first time SW19 had shown its true hip hop credibility as Move-Bustin' American rap icon Young MC was born just down the road in South Wimbledon. He later headed to Queens, one of New York's toughest boroughs, and musical hotbeds, as opposed to the genteel grass court tournament in nearby Kensington.

MURRAY'S MINT

Most of the Brits did the polite thing and followed leading man Henman straight out of the tournament but world No.169 Andrew Murray, clad fittingly in Fred Perry clothing, had other ideas. He caused quite a stir at the tender age of 17 as he strode past Sampras Surpriser George Bastl in only his fifth professional match, before unbelievably dispatching wily No.14 seed, Radek Stepanek, with similar ease in the next round. The papers lost the plot, mocking up an image of him with the trophy and talking up the fact that his fist pumps were more 'purposeful' than poor old Tim's. BB chimed in with the most specific prediction of all[52] when he said that he thought Murray could win the 2012 Olympics gold.

The dream lasted another couple of days before the young hero went down in five agonising sets to previous finalist David Nalbandian. Clearly exhausted (he'd never played five sets before), the papers set him up as the gritty, non-snooty Wimbledon Real Deal and the heir to Fred Perry's working-class hero crown. This was only helped when Wimblephile Sean Connery energetically got behind his countryman in the stadium, leading to headlines such as the brilliant, 'YOU ONLY SERVE TWICE', to the awful 'DR NO TIE BREAK IN THE FIFTH SET'[1].

JOLLY ROGER

Elsewhere, the superlatives were flowing like cheap rum aboard the good ship Jolly Roger as he was described as an artist, ice-cool, Borgian, a genius, Leonardo da Vinci, a legend and the GOAT.[53] His rhythm, flow and tempo were making the world purr and after crushing Hewitt in the semi-final he made short work of likeable US jock (and Stifler from *American Pie* lookalike) Andy Roddick in the final, barely breaking sweat. John McEnroe was fast becoming the GOAT of the commentary box, with his incisive and informed observations, and led the merry band of swashbuckling Fed fans. That's enough of the pirate thing.

---

52 And weirdly spot on.

53 GOAT is the acronym used in various sports for Greatest Of All Time. Unofficially owned by Muhammad Ali.

Ladies' Champion *Venus Williams*
Gentlemen's Champion *Roger Federer*

ROOFLESS TENNIS

Work on the new, retractable, roof had started by lopping off the old one, leaving the 84-year-old stadium looking like a Roman amphitheatre, as if we had all journeyed back in history. The Club announced that this new roof project would take a lengthy three years, which is the amount of time it takes to go to Mars and back, or complete an honours degree in biomedical science.

LONDON FASHION WEEKS

This was the year when fashion really hit SW19 as, for the first time since Suzanne Lenglen, or certainly Ted Tinling[li], the ensembles were making all the headlines. New press darling and Russian sweetheart, Maria Kirilenko, rocked up in an outfit designed by Stella McCartney and the press talked more about ruffles, pleats, ra-ras and layers than they did volleys and backhands. She lost in the first round. American Bethanie Mattek was less elegant, and more extravagant, in her choice of 70s skater socks, a boob tube, a tiny vest and chandelier earrings, described as 'a soccer theme', to general bemusement as *The Guardian* likened it to 'a discarded PE kit'. She won one game in losing emphatically to Venus Williams in the first round. The men were not to be outdone as show pony Roger Federer reverse overhead smashed back the idea that fashion flamboyance is just for the ladies. He proved it by inventing the 'walk-on jacket', a highfalutin' cream blazer bearing his name and three trophy icons, in case we'd forgotten how many Championships he'd already won.

Even the officials got in on the regalia act as the rumoured £10 million tie-in with Ralph Lauren[54] was unveiled, in more ways than one. The tighty whitey Ralphy trousers had to be recalled as splits were reported in 60 of the 335 pairs, leading to unsightly shots of middle-aged men departing courts holding their bottoms.

BELIEVE THE UNBELIEVABLE

David Foster Wallace, the revered American novelist, essayist and all-round genius, once said, 'Tennis' beauty's infinite roots are self-competitive. You compete with your own limits to transcend the self in imagination and execution.' He followed this throwaway observation with a study called 'Roger

---

54 To create what David Foster Wallace called 'children's navalwear', adding 'fashion critic' to his lengthy CV.

Federer As Religious Experience', as if the Swiss virtuoso needed any more confidence-building. The new essay all but canonised Federer, citing a mixture of kinaesthetic ability, human beauty and metaphysics, and describing him as 'like something out of *The Matrix*'.

DESPERATE TIMS

Henman was now down at No.59 in the world and had the unenviable task of taking on The Religious Experience and his Crowd Disciples in the second round. It was as emphatic as we had feared. A young Serbian, and sometime Andrew Murray doubles partner, by the name of Novak Djokovic, announced his arrival and coquettishly revealed that he had approached the LTA about the possibility of his family moving here, thus taking up British citizenship. He revealed that everyone's favourite adopted Brit, Greg Rusedski, had constantly been joshing with him in the locker room, repeatedly greeting him with that much-loved British phrase everyone uses, 'What's up, British?' Novak's Mum, downright nationality-flirt Dijana, sipped Guinness courtside with journalists and observed, while gazing into the distance with a teasing grin, that, 'Great Britain is looking for heroes.' Who isn't?

UNICORNS AND CHEESE

On the first Tuesday Bally and I reunited for the first time in years and found ourselves next to the poshest people we had ever met in The Queue, even in life. We watched with wonder as the couple, in their 60s, unpacked what looked like the arrival tent for a county fair from a nearby parked Land Rover Defender. 'Right', said the Lady of the Manor, 'Move those blankets over there darling,' to a slightly out-of-breath, but cheery, older gent. 'Not there darling … I don't want to make a fuss, but I want them here.' They continued to unload a small wicker factory, pausing to set up the most important part – the camping hob. 'Put the kettle on, darling,' was heard four times in the first hour. They introduced themselves as 'Harvey and Ripples', and we were immediately fascinated. 'We're from Colston Bassett, you know, like the cheese?' We admitted that we didn't know of the world-famous Stilton-producing town and in less than five minutes Ripples had served us some, on crackers, with a chilled glass of white.

It turned out that Rippleton was their surname, hence the lady's nickname (we were never told the real one), as the cheese was followed by homemade Scotch eggs.

'I'm in a bit of a pickle, Ripples,' panted Harvey, as he struggled with the mechanics of a military chair dating back to the Battle of Agincourt. 'You'll get there, darling,' Ripples breezily informed him as he trapped his fingers in the cast iron hinge and muffled 'Oh bugger…Sod it…Bollocks' into his handkerchief.

'It's funny really as Harvey's father still has debenture tickets on Centre, hardly ever uses them.'

Our mouths were open in disbelief.

'My bloody fingers are stuck, Ripples.'

'Don't make such a fuss, darling. You know, we're British, we're all a bit nutty, aren't we? At the end of the day we've all got bloody unicorns on our passports.' A fact I had never noticed and would now never forget.

WE'VE REACHED A ROUNDABOUT IN OUR RELATIONSHIP

That visit was the last time that Bally and I attended The Championships together, after which he moved away for a teaching job and we simply drifted apart. I actually remember us parting ways at the roundabout in Wimbledon village that evening – he headed to one pub to meet his friends and I headed to the one down the road to meet mine. We must have passed that intersection 50 times together over the years, either full of excitement on the way down, or cream-crackered on the way back up. We shook hands and agreed to hook up at Christmas, a plan we both knew we wouldn't stick to. He made a joke about Murray, and how he would never win it, and I joked about his favourite, Federer, turning barley water into wine. And then we both went our separate ways, disappearing into the respective pub throngs outside the two old Wimbledon village institutions. I remember this parting moment, of the passing of childhood friendship, as being soundtracked by the theme tune to *Whatever Happened to the Likely Lads?*[55], in my head.

THE COMIC EFFECT

Number one-ranked Brit, Andrew Murray, continued to rise but experienced the full brunt of a media backlash when royally stitched up by Tim Henman in a joint interview. Henman was taking the mickey out of Scotland's national football team's pedigree and Murray responded by suggesting his chosen team to support in the upcoming Scotland-free World Cup would be, 'Anyone that's playing England.' Middle England went nuts, particularly on radio phone-ins, as it was revealed that he was receiving a torrent of abuse on his Twitter account.

Another night in The Queue certainly backed this up as his throwaway banter seemed to have stirred the lack of humour in the country as a whole. One bumptious older gent firmly informed me, as he pointed at the grounds for clarity, 'It's called the blinking All England Club, not the "All Britain Club".' A patriotic bloke wearing a vintage Argentina football shirt I met whilst having a pee in a portaloo said solemnly,

---

55 The song is called 'Whatever Happened To You?' and still makes me teary to this day. I am pleased to say that the writing of this book put us back into contact, and not just on Facebook. I must play him the song.

'They should ban him from playing.' Golf's serial non-winner of major trophies, fellow Scot Colin Montgomerie, 'warned' Murray to 'cool it'.

THERE'S SOMETHING HAPPENING HERE

As temperatures soared the country was flooded with standard summer fayre; ball girls collapsing at Wimbledon, supposed great white (that turned out to be basking) sharks terrorising Cornish beaches and England crashing out of a big football tournament with a flood of tears and recrimination and a slo-mo 'highlights' film, set to some mopey Britpop guitar track. World No.3 seed Andy Roddick was Murray's mountain to climb in the third round and, in a flawless tactical performance, climb he did, leaving the bitter naysayers behind. Dismantling Roddick's incredible serve, Murray revealed that lucky Bond charm Connery had called, and presumably inspired, him the night before. It was easily the most exciting thing to happen in British tennis since Henman knocked out the ball girl.

The brouhaha was soon cooled when Murray went down in straight sets to Baghdatis, but it felt very much like a star had been born. Djokovic was somewhat harshly described as a 'British let down'[lii] in the press, when he wasn't even British yet, probably cementing his decision to park that 'changing nationality' idea before it went much further.

FASHION FINALE

The style-conscious and entertaining fortnight reached its crescendo as Sir Cliff wore an emetic salmon pink blazer and twinned it with an optic neuritis-inducing[56] animal print shirt for his day in the Royal Box. Roger Federer made it a fifth

---

56 An inflammation of the nerve that travels from the back of the eyeball into your brain.

straight final in Major events by dispatching Swede Jonas Bjorkman for the loss of just four games, no break points, and seemingly not one drop of sweat. In fact he seemed to exert more sweat in signing the giant Slazenger tennis balls kids were now thrusting in his way on exiting the court – a new, and completely brilliant, merchandising addition this year.

Waiting in the final was the Pirata himself, the man who had beaten him in six of their last seven meetings, including the recent French Open Final. Federer was still the king of grass and he won his fourth straight Wimbledon final in four sets. I remember the match more for how often Rafa used a towel between points, casually throwing the sweat-soaked cloth straight back at his ~~personal valet~~ ball boy/girl like something out of the Dark Ages, when we used children for hard, dirty labour. For the ladies, charming Frenchwoman Amélie Mauresmo conquered her occasional nerves on the big stage to make for a popular champion.

REALITY STAR

Dimitry Tursunov, previous Henman conqueror and as mad as a March hare, delivered the quote of the year when he was quizzed about hitting the ball in the general direction of the umpire, Fergus Murphy. 'If I had been hitting at him, I would have hit him. Not the bottom of the chair. The guy's an idiot. Just because he's been umpiring for many years doesn't mean that he's been doing a good job. Saddam Hussein has been in Iraq for a while, but not too many people agree with his point of view.'[57] It was hard to contradict such a venomous defence.

---

57 The scalding heat of his statement was only exceeded by Lighton Ndefwayl, a Zambian tennis player, in 1992. Ndefwayl stated in defeat, 'Musumba Bwayla is a stupid man and a hopeless player. He has a huge nose and is cross-eyed. Girls hate him. He beat me because my jockstrap was too tight and because when he serves, he farts, and that made me lose the concentration for which I am famous throughout Zambia.'

Ladies' Champion *Amélie Mauresmo*
Gentlemen's Champion *Roger Federer*

UNDERCRACKERS

Wimbledon encourages a sizeable fascination with undergarments. In recent times I blame the legendary Athena poster of the woman scratching her bum for linking forever the tennis court and the human bottom. Or maybe it's just our national obsession with the seaside postcard.

1. Trailblazing flapper **Suzanne Lenglen** kicked it all off in the 1920s, changing women's tennis attire for good, and influencing fashion in the broadest sense. Ditching the corset, the petticoat, the suspenders and the sleeves gave her the pinchy nickname 'The French hussy' on Wimbledon's modest lawns.

2. Even as astute a tennis observer as the legendary Fred Perry himself noted in his autobiography that, 'When **Billie Tapscott** went on Centre Court with no stockings she caused a furore.' It was 1927, and easier to shock.

3. Londoner **Joan Austin** ditched her stockings in 1931 and a year later her brother Bunny joined her in revolution, thus becoming the first man to wear shorts at a proper tournament. He was also the last British man to get to a Wimbledon final before Andy Murray, who also wore shorts.

4. **'Gorgeous Gussie' Moran** shocked fans and delighted the papers when she rocked up at Wimbledon in 1949 wearing a shorter skirt over frilly, lace-trimmed knickers. Despite losing in the first round (a recurrent theme for the undercracker pioneer) she was criticised for bringing 'vulgarity and sin into tennis'. She probably didn't read the critics as she was too busy appearing on the fronts of magazines, having an aircraft named after her and dating very wealthy men*.

5. **Karol Short** wore gold lamé underpants in 1958, at least 19 years before Studio 54 opened, and 43 years before Ms Minogue slipped hers on. She had trialled the showy little

numbers the month before at the more liberal French Open, but right here in Blighty they were banned outright, for fear that they might put an opponent off.

6. **Linda Siegel** completely forgot her bra when playing Billie Jean King in the second round in 1979. The 18-year-old Californian came out of the top of her halterneck dress, explaining 'everything just fell out'. The *Daily Telegraph* declared, sombrely, 'Miss Siegel, needing to make some essential adjustments; did not learn the strategic value of a pin.' The *Daily Mirror* screamed, 'bra-less, backless and as she admitted later, a bit reckless'. Mrs King put it best, 'If endowed, wear it.'

7. The 1970s and 1980s was a global boom period for tennis and the men, not wanting to be left out of this fabric-slashing revolution, raised their hemlines by a good three inches. **Björn, Jimmy and John**** led the way with some serious bot-skimming hot-pant action, and Ivan and Boris were only too happy to follow suit in the next decade.

8. Frenchwoman **Tatiana Golovin** strode on to court in 2007 and proceeded to show the world her knickers. This would not have been noteworthy other than for the fact that they were strawberry red. Sadly Golovin would only last a couple of rounds but promised more in the undercracker department, menacingly stating that she had 'something crazy planned' for some future date with her controversial destiny***. The tabloids had a field day.

---

* Sadly, in 2004 it was reported that 80-year-old Gussie Moran was forced to sell off her knickers on eBay to save herself from destitution.
** They sound like a Scandinavian Eurovision Song Contest entry.
*** The world is still waiting on tenterhooks at the time of writing.

GREAT EXPECTATIONS

In the previous year Andrew, now shortened to the much more easy-going 'Andy', Murray had broken Roger Federer's 55-match hard court winning streak, joining Rafael Nadal as one of only two men to beat him all year, also winning his first ATP event. Hopes were high coming into the tournament but the Gods went and served up the wettest Wimbledon on record, which would eventually end on the fifth Thursday. It was not just meteorologically wet, it also became a damp squib for Brit fans when Murray was forced to pull out the day before the start, having failed to recover from a wrist injury six weeks before. 'GRIMBLEDON', groaned about three tabloids.

ALL MEN, AND NOW WOMEN, ARE EQUAL.
BUT SOME MEN ARE STILL A BIT MORE EQUAL

2007 was the year when the Club caught up with the changing times and awarded the ladies the same prize money as the gents. Chairman Tim Phillips announced that, 'The time is right to bring this subject to a logical conclusion and eliminate the difference … In short, good for tennis, good for women players and good for Wimbledon.' The sporting world applauded and Venus Williams gushed, 'The greatest tennis tournament in the world has reached an even greater height today.' With parity now universal, it did still seem strange that the men still 'opened' and 'closed' Major tournaments with the blue ribbon events, which should surely be alternated every year for full equality?

SUITS HIM

After a previous Wimbledon which was almost entirely taken over by fashion, the rag trade started to really get a taste for the event in 2007. The Artist Formerly Known As Roger, now boasting ten Major titles, actually walked on water as he arrived on a dreary and damp Centre Court on the opening day, dressed as a kind of celestial waiter-cum-naval officer, in a pristine ivory warm-up suit.

BLEAK HOUSE

For the nation, annual hope and expectation now shifted back to Tim, who had all but stopped playing competitively at the age of 33. In a sterling effort to raise the national mood he served up a nostalgic reminder of days gone by as he battled through a five-set classic with Carlos Moya, in his favoured tea-time-into-twilight slot, eventually triumphing 13-11 in the fifth and beaming on court with the abandon of a man with a weight lifted from his shoulders. As the game went on Sue Barker sounded almost wistful when she delivered her customary, 'We're going to stay with the tennis here on BBC1, if you'd like to watch the news please switch over to …' He went down in the second round to the devilishly handsome Feliciano Lopez, but again in a more than respectable five sets.

The rest of British tennis reached an all-time low, Henman himself deriding the no-hopers with the extremely appropriate 'gutless' label, after only one other player got through the first round.

EYE OF THE STORM

The all-new computer system finally arrived, to replace the much-maligned, and badly named, 'Cyclops' one. Cyclops had been famed for its Dr Who-like infa-red beams and the fact that it only had one eye, which was surely inferior to the two most humans have? The new 'Hawkeye' (they should have named it 'Hawkeyes', much sexier and also multi-eyed) system had been successfully used in cricket, and at other tournaments, before getting this, the big gig. Hawkeye had been frequently mentioned (longingly) during the French Open, where they use the less technical 'point-animatedly-at-the-mark-you-think-the-ball-made-then-have-a-big-row' system. Making a billion calculations per second from ten on-court cameras, fans were transfixed, which was just as well as there was not much going on elsewhere at SW19, and it cemented the feeling that the line calls were the more interesting spectacle.

DRIPS AND DRAB

My own queuing was limited to the diurnal as I decided that 62°F in the daytime would not create the Mediterranean-style camping experience I was after. On one of the days I attended, when I am pretty sure I had mild frostbite, I was next to a group of ladies from Brighton who proudly told me that they were attending with the main objective of trying to get a glimpse of David Beckham in the Royal Box, with any tennis 'a bonus'.

The absence of star power from a Brit POV was a factor in making it feel flat, as was the continuing abysmal weather, the worst since 1982, with lightning literally stopping play at one point. It seemed like the Beeb had Sue Barker on loop saying, as cameras panned from St Mary's Church to the common, 'Well that's the scene right now here at Wimbledon. Let's switch our thoughts back to last year's final when Roger Federer ...' When a ball boy slid on a greasy court and ended up bandaged from a collision with an air blower it seemed to sum it all up. It was also revealed that the (insanely bored) players were struggling with the Club's £23 daily food allowance, but were more than enjoying the offer of free pairs of West End theatre tickets. Most likely for *Les Misérables*.

BRIT WINS WIMBLEDON!

The papers cheered, in a slightly ironic way, as Andy's older brother, Jamie, won the mixed doubles with Jelena Janković, becoming the first Brit in 20 years outside of the catering corps to hold some silverware at SW19. The doubles game had changed considerably in recent years, primarily as the top players seemed to have opted out en masse. John McEnroe, who played doubles in part to replace training sessions, and Pat Cash had been on opposite sides of the net in the '84 final, Graf and Sabatini won it in '88, Martina always played it, so did Martina Hingis, but only the Williams sisters had regularly participated in recent years. It had become an almost separate discipline for 'doubles specialists', who were normally players we didn't know well from the singles scene. It seemed a great shame as the doubles game was often less intense (the tension shared between two) and allowed you to see the top players' personalities a bit more, which was mostly a good thing. Just don't ask Tim Henman.

HEAVY IS THE HEAD THAT WEARS THE CROWN?

Apparently not. Federer copied Borg, winning five on the bounce, after a classic with an increasingly grass-friendly Nadal. 'Now he knows the game on grass much better,' Federer said, barely disguising an antsy look over his warm-down blazer's shoulder-pad. Serena Williams provided the insightful moments when, during a match against Daniela Hanutchova, she was photographed reading the most simplistic self-help notes ever seen, 'You R No.1', 'My good thoughts are powerful, any negative thoughts are weak' were only topped by the most direct of all, borrowed from a primary school pencil case circa 1982, 'You are the best'. It proved strangely incorrect as big sister Venus, and not her, went on to win her fourth title.

Ladies' Champion *Venus Williams*
Gentlemen's Champion *Roger Federer*

HOW *NOT* TO DRESS FOR WIMBLEDON

PART 2: LADIES

There's more fun to be had for women on a day out at the tennis, as generally the fairer sex look less ridiculous when embracing fashion and 'making an effort'. But let's not get too carried away, there are still some rules which need to be adhered to.

1. Avoid tennis ball earrings or headbands – you may get your photograph in the paper, but you will regret it down the line. In fact, just avoid ironic use of fluo yellow felt in general.

2. Plastic fruit as an added detail to an outfit is not something you would consider in most situations, so Wimbledon should be no different. And a fake strawberry on a hat is the kind of thing a five-year-old would struggle to pull off with any credibility.

3. Union Jacks have no place on your person, especially not on your fingernails.

4. Straw trilbys and fedoras have already been questioned for men, so there is no reason to approach this any differently for women.

5. White jeans are fine, as long as you are either 18, or your name is 'Elizabeth Hurley'.

6. Face paint is unbecoming, and the smaller the design, the worse it is. So either go big or go home. Or just don't go to Wimbledon.

7. As with men you should avoid any overtly tennis-themed attire. If you are thinking about pulling out that old lacey, racy Teddy Tinling babydoll number you last wore in 1982, think again, we live in different times.

8. Business-style skirt suits are tricky. On the one hand they are chic and classy, but on the other hand you are not Tracy Austin.

9. Anything with piping is to be avoided. It can be embarrassing to get mistaken for a line judge.

10. An official-looking t-shirt bought from the shop on the grounds is a great addition to your wardrobe, but don't actually wear it to the tennis, unless you want to be inundated by people asking you where the left luggage office is.

THE ROARING NOUGHTIES

In the year that I moved from one side of London to the other, and into a flat practically overlooking the Wimbledon practice courts, the new roof had finally been put in place and was almost ready for action. The 'Roaring Twenties' were trending everywhere, with women in shorts (tabloid groan audible), but also blazers and tutus.

Roger arrived at SW19 on the back of an almighty spanking in the Roland Garros final at the hands of Rafa, but on the plus side he had a brand new Jay Gatsby-inspired outfit for the occasion, his shoes and canvas belt both adorned with a trophy icon and the number '5'. I was half-expecting The Fine Fedsby to walk out on the Monday in Nike spats, braces, a Panama hat and a pocket watch. He was probably hosting extravagant nightly parties at a giant mansion on the edge of Wimbledon Common. Serena showed up wearing a mackintosh, explaining it with, 'I live in Florida and I probably have more coats than anybody', which didn't make sense on any level. Commercial golden girls (leggy, white, beponytailed, only occasionally successful) Maria and Ana

Ivanovic looked the part, Maria in a kind of bib and tucker, or tuxedo shirt, but it was (Kournik)over a bit quickly as they were both out by the end of the first week.

GREEN SHOOTS OF CHANGE

The Queue was now officially tested in the singular as the two separate entities, Church and Somerset Roads, merged into one and the whole thing found itself in Wimbledon Park, the Capability Brown-designed expanse of field next to the golf course. You couldn't help but wonder if legendary landscape architect Brown had dialled this project's design in a bit, what with it not being landscaped very much and just being a big field with a lake next to it. It was announced that a new legal agreement would keep the fans 'off the streets of SW19', making us sound like a bunch of ASBOs, and the All England Club made the official agreement with Merton Council to move The Queue to the park.

'It's like a holiday camp!' the man next to me cheerily observed as he arrived on the first Wednesday. It was, if you would be pleased with a burger stall, a giant portaloo and view of a fence for your vacation experience. But the great thing about the new set-up was the overall cosiness of sleeping by a giant bank of poplar and cypress trees, and far away from a busy road. I also particularly enjoyed the new official 'Guide To Queuing' pamphlet being distributed, which made the suggestion that you 'settle down' at around 10pm. As a nostalgic grown-up this made me, a Queuer, feel like a child, with the HSs wandering around like the adults. I almost asked to be read a story.

On the other side I had a kindly gent who politely informed me that he had booked a B&B down the road but assured me that he would only 'pop over there at 4am to have a shower and a shave, and put some slacks on'. I graciously agreed, in no small part because I love people who call trousers 'slacks'. When he came back at 5am he looked like he had been on some kind of makeover programme, while I looked like I had been sleeping in a park all night. Fun CampBoy on the other side grinned maniacally and gurned, 'Queuing is fun!' at the crack of dawn, whilst scoffing from a bag of mini chicken Kievs. Later on, at the end of the day, I bumped into him in another queue, this time back at the left luggage, 'Haha, it's like Hedgehog Day!' he guffawed, smelling a little 'foody'. I was actually growing to quite like him.

GOODBYE, HELLO

British tennis said goodbye to 'Tiger' Tim – the greatest Briton we had seen for 30 years – who got to No.4 in the world and was now commentating for the BBC, doing a great impression of a commentator very much in his own image. His first appearance in the booth saw him start well, go off the boil as everyone got in from work, become jittery about tea-time and then just about come through in the end, to great national relief. The country said a big hello to smiley 14-year-old British rising star, Laura Robson, who was inexplicably labelled a 'Spice Girl', and then, after winning the Girls' singles title, had her odds of winning the big one by 2020 slashed to 50-1[liii].

BEFORE ROGER, WE HAD OUR OWN ROGER

I met some completely dotty older ladies in The Queue who wore their love for Roger loud and proud. Just not that Roger. Older British tennis fans always talk fondly of Roger Taylor, not the drummer out of Queen, but the Yorkshire-born star of the 60s and 70s who knocked out Rod Laver on his way to his second Wimbledon semi-final. Taylor was a handsome devil, a kind of swarthy proto-Rog, a dashing, dark swordsmith who slashed his way to the hearts of housewives all over Britain. 'We used to see him in the grounds and he'd always say hello, with a wink. And then if he talked to you, you literally melted.' I doubted the latter, but could see the point.

I'M STRONG TO THE FIN-ICH, CAUSE I EATS ME SPIN-ACH

Andy Murray rocked up in fine form in 2008, looking as fit as a butcher's dog, up to No.11 in the world and taking on the Middle England doubters with a gruff comment and a fierce forehand. I was pretty chuffed to see my old friend from home, Matt Little, who had been working with the LTA, now a part of Murray's team on the fitness side. In some weird way I felt this was a good omen. He was certainly getting more out of The Future Of British Tennis than he did out of me.

Murray wasted no time in informing the country, 'I am not anti-English ... I am Scottish. I am also British ... my girlfriend is English, my gran Shirley – who I love to bits – is English.' It was both emphatic and authoritative, and his gran Shirley beamed proudly, whilst his girlfriend must have been left feeling somewhat confused about the pecking order. That said, the nation expected, and if they could forgive Tim for almost decapitating a schoolgirl then there was hope for Andy. Murray reached the fourth round impressively, then came from two sets down to beat Richard Gasquet in one of Centre Court's modern classics. A good dose of grit, great touch, a couple of 'highlights reel' points and a Popeye impression after one of them, flexing his significantly larger bicep, captured the nation. Then he came up against the original Bicep Boy himself, Rafa, in the quarters and was swatted aside with ease.

SCRUMPY GLEN

In The Queue at the start of the second week I found myself next to a cheery fellow from Warwickshire called Glen who I remember for the fact that he still called his mobile a 'carphone'[58], as well as his prodigious drinking. He didn't stop quaffing unbranded bottles of cider all day, which turned out to be made by a friend of his, and I watched with fascination as, completely inebriated, he breezily attempted to bash his tent pegs into the hard ground with the palm of his hand. He offered me a bottle and in the space of about 15 minutes I felt heady, then delirious, then more happy than I had ever been in my life and finally so sad that I wanted to cry uncontrollably. I declined further refreshment but Glen kept going. At about 9pm he went for a walk and I was slightly concerned when he got back to see him completely soaked to the bone, as it wasn't raining. 'Fell in the boating lake,' he said, as if it was the most normal thing in the world. 'Did it last year as well.' I smiled nervously, said my goodnights and fastened my tent door securely.

A FAMILY AFFAIR

Venus and Serena seemed to be just about the best thing to happen to women's tennis in years; their non-posh, non-

---

58 You could level the same criticism at 'Carphone Warehouse', and it doesn't seem to have done them any harm.

middle-class, non-white trailblazing opening the game up wider than it had ever been and taking it to a whole new audience. Their incredible success was still leading to audible grumbles about their increasing dominance, as opposed to bemoaning the lack of any credible, consistent challenge from elsewhere. 2008 saw them meet for the third time in the final – Venus claiming this one, for her first against Serena.

I was a big fan of Venus and her style of play but also thoroughly enjoyed the sense of high camp/drama, often self-created, which surrounded Serena wherever she went. If you could honestly say that you would prefer to watch a couple of faceless, personality-less, blonde ponytails[59] thrashing and screeching around from the baseline than Serena in her pomp then you'd be mad. Or a tabloid editor.

GLOOM, AND BOOM!

With the roof on, but still not active, Gentlemen's Finals Day looked worryingly like being spoilt by the rain. The rumoured Nadal hex on Federer seemed to be getting to the Prince Regent of Wimbledon, but no one quite saw this one coming, as a perfect clash of styles came together to create the perfect drama, much like Borg and McEnroe in 1980. Even their personalities matched up well; Federer all Zen, sweat-free and calm focus, Rafa nervy, dripping in perspiration, his repertoire of obsessive and compulsive superstitions and habits there for all to see. At 9.20pm, with the court practically pitch black, Nadal won his first non-Parisian Major title. He said, when serving for the match at 8-7, 'I couldn't see a thing', but sportingly referred to Roger as 'still the best'. It was a debate everyone was having, and my money was on a changing of the guard, with Rafa the ascendant. Just don't ask him if he turned the iron off.

---

59 It always strikes me as strange that there are so few short-haired female tennis players. Far less than the percentage in real life. Aerodynamically, there must be an advantage to having less of it in the way?

Ladies' Champion *Venus Williams*
Gentlemen's Champion *Rafael Nadal*

ROOF RAISER

The roof was unveiled in May with a peculiar exhibition match featuring husband and wife Andre Agassi and Steffi Graf, playing the rather random pairing of Tim Henman and Kim Clijsters. Tennis exhibition matches are decidedly uncool, with most players not doubling up as stand-up comedians, and the 'banter' tends to be firmly set at 'cringe'. This one did not disappoint, with most of the crowd cracking up like schoolkids every time Agassi kissed Graf, which he did about 80 times.[60]

The proper tennis was only days in before the £80 million Centre Court roof construction started being questioned, as temperatures soared and previously sodden fans were praised for 'braving the heat'. How quickly we forget.

The Parisian spring had seen Duc Roger de Basel complete his 'career Grand Slam' by winning the French Open against

---

60 One exception to this was the Sampras/Federer v Agassi/Nadal exhibition for the Haiti earthquake tragedy, in which a testy Agassi insulted Sampras for being mean with tipping and the atmosphere was painfully awkward throughout. Nadal grinned nervously, like someone not entirely sure what two foreign people were arguing about, while Roger 'Berlitz' Federer smiled nervously, like someone who really did.

Robin Söderling, who had moved that blessed (and probably injured) Rafa out of his way. Nadal would also not be in SW19, leaving the door wide open once again for Federer. On a more local front the papers[liv] were full of rumours that Murray was seeking the 'advice' of non-major-international-tournament-winning David Beckham in 'handling the pressure'. Hmmm.

POP CULTURE

With a 50-date residency looming at the O2 Arena, the Dark Lord of Pop, Michael Jackson, was pronounced dead after collapsing at his rented home in Los Angeles. Never one to miss a link, a BBC commentator actually said, 'How fitting if today, Roger Federer, the King of Wimbledon, has the honour of being the first to play under the Centre Court roof, on the day after the passing of the King of Pop.'[lv] There were so many conditions on the observation that the whole country lost track. Serena Williams gushed over the Moonwalker's departure, saying, 'He was the celebrity of all celebrities ... iconic on every level.' She talked of her awe at meeting him and how much of an impression he made on her. When pressed on her favourite Jacko song she said, 'I don't remember the name of it. It's a slower one.'

THE GRUNT IS BACK

After being booed off court at the French Open the shrieking, and brilliantly named, Michele Larcher de Brito hit the previously unthinkable 109 decibel level – the same as a Formula One car – as her agents warned her to drop it down a few gears. Gisele Dulko saw off previous Queen Gruntress Maria Sharapova in the second round as the Russian, increasingly getting headlines for her attire rather than her results, came dressed as an all-white tribute to one of those wooden Christmas soldiers who bang drums, minus the majorette hat. Dulko was officially deemed 'Not Hard To Look At', so the papers went nuts about the 'New Queen of Wimbledon'. She lost in the next round.

SELF-DEFEATING

Fifteen-year-old junior champ Laura Robson came a cropper in the first round of the grown-up competition, prompting her Mum to put all the blame on the intense studying programme she had been following for her recent GCSEs. It's admittedly hard to achieve in top-tier sport when you are trying to remember how an ox-bow lake is formed and the employment of the French pluperfect tense.

Anne Keothavong, the likeable, and at No.51 in the world, respectably performing, Brit female star, imploded on court and then repeated it in her almost unwatchably brutal self-assessment in the interview room. By round two there were only two Brits standing. Yawn.

HONOUR AMONGST THIEVES

It was leaked to the press that 2,000 official towels had been nicked from the locker rooms, with the players and, in some cases, their entourages, the number one suspects. The Wimbledon police announced that they were on the lookout for athletes showing no sign of dampness under their all-whites, leading to some jittery glances in the Federer camp.

TURNING THE TIDE

Murray was now beating the top players all the time, as he rose to a lofty No.3 in the world. He had just become the first British winner of Queen's since 1938 and even received a congratulatory letter from the actual Queen, possibly confused by the name of the event and thinking that she owned it. It was now 73 years and counting since our last male champion but Andy stormed through to the third round in style, like a man on a mission.

I queued overnight for the next match, listening in to a number of enlightening Murray-themed conversations. This was one, between a very Middle England husband and wife, which I actually scribbled down in line:

- Do you like this Murray lad, Lynn?
Yes, I think so, as a player. But I don't know really? Do you think I would like him? He's British, isn't he?
- Yes. Well he's Scottish, so sort of British.
He doesn't sound Scottish. Does he?
- I think he does. He can also seem terribly glum, so he probably is. But I suppose he does have the whole weight of a nation on his shoulders.
The Scottish nation?

- No, the British nation. Well, the British Isles. I read in
the paper that he watches that show *Mock The Week*,
so he must have a bit of a sense of humour.
I don't know what that is.
- You don't know what a 'sense of humour' is?
No, Mockney Week.
- It's called *Mock The Week*.
*I think I do like him, he's terribly good at tennis. I remember
now, he likes his Mum. I read that. And he listens to her.
You can tell that.*
- I agree, he's a good sort all round.
*I wonder if he likes porridge? All the Scottish like that. Do you
think if he wins he'll wave a saltire flag?*
- If he wins Wimbledon I don't care if he waves a blooming
swastika flag.

INTO THE GROOVE

The overall anti-Murray tide did seem to be turning slowly,
with a fair amount of people talking about his sharp sense of
humour, as well as his refreshing candour in interviews. The
hype was cemented by an incredible five-set thriller against
Stan 'The Man' Wawrinka in the fourth round, which
became the first match to be played entirely under the roof,
and the latest ever SW19 finish, at 10.40pm.[61]

Inside the newly modernised stadium the electric
atmosphere felt completely fresh, the floodlights adding a
dramatic tension as the ball fizzed under the lights, each rifle
shot of a groundstroke whipcracking in the air, adrenalin
dripping off the roof. Who knew whether or not Murray was
going to ever get there, but it felt like things were changing,
and I was pretty sure I liked it.

---

61 I have never been able to see Stan's full name, Stanislas Wawrinka, without
thinking how it fits perfectly in time with the chorus of Madonna's 'La Isla
Bonita', 'This is where I want to be … Stan-ees-laz, Vav-reeenka.'

We poured out on to the hill after the match, a stiflingly warm night in spite of the rain, which was still packed with huge crowds who'd stayed in near darkness to watch. It felt magical. Days later Andy reached a first semi-final and the nation held its breath as he faced up to the very beatable (for him) Andy Roddick. They split a couple of sets before two tense tie-breaks saw Andy hit his head on the roof of Roddick's prodigious grass court game. It was an epic 'ANDY CLIMAX'[lvi] and the players departed with Roddick, ever the gent, mouthing, 'I'm sorry' to the watching British fans. Some of the more defeatist press responded as if that was it for Murray, and hadn't he put up a jolly good fight in the slightly naïve 'trying to win Wimbledon' thing. They also didn't seem all that disappointed that he hadn't.

GET YOUR COAT
Another all-Williams final was nicknamed 'YAWN ON THE FOURTH OF JULY'[lvii], Serena coming through in straight sets for her 11th big one. Federer and Roddick played the longest Wimbledon final in history with Federer winning 16-14 in the fifth set, the last game the only time Roddick had his serve broken, winning his 15th Major in front of the watching Pete Sampras. In victory he unveiled his new gold-braided jacket, which he had ready in his bag, adorned with the number '15'. It turned out that a Nike exec had passed the jacket to him after the match, but it still felt a bit puffed up, and a shade disrespectful to Roddick. One couldn't help but wonder if the Beau Brummell of tennis had another one with '14' stitched on in case he had lost.

Ladies' Champion *Serena Williams*
Gentlemen's Champion *Roger Federer*

FINE LINES

In January Andy Murray got to another Major final, in Australia, and again lost in straight sets, again to that dastardly Mr Federer. The New Queue at the AELTC now got the full Glastonbury seal of approval as the unforgiving pavements were officially supplanted by the green grass of the park and proper tents (poles, pegs … just tents, basically) replaced the makeshift tarpaulin hut villages. Chief executive Ian Ritchie dropped one of the Club's well-timed, inclusive statements when he said, 'The Wimbledon Queue has become a legendary part of The Championships.'

The weather for once behaved, with temperatures in the high 80s, which was hotter, as we were always informed as if it were a competition, than both Rhodes and the Costa del Sol. I slept out in sub-tropical heat on the first night and met a born-again Christian, called Royston, who was wearing a slick t-shirt printed with an image of Jesus wearing shades like Arnie in *The Terminator*, accompanied by the message, 'I'LL BE BACK'. At about 6am he just got up and left, seemingly satisfied with the Queue experience. He never did come back, but he was probably there in spirit.

GOOD MORNING, GOOD MORNING

Waking up that morning at 5-something, as the sun rose behind the park treeline, I felt overwhelmed by the thrilling spectacle. Hundreds, now thousands, of diverse people with one collective desire, pulling in the same direction, a tingle of anticipation in the already warm air as the excited chatter of the early arrivers mingled with the sleepy stirring of the all-nighters, tripping over guide ropes as they made their way to the loos. Newspaper vendors started their rounds and Honorary Stewards gently tapped on the tents with the politest alarm calls possible, as the day broke in our weird sporting camp. There could be no question about it, The Queue was the true heartbeat of modern Wimbledon.

Just an hour later and the somnolent park was transformed into a vibrant mass of zealots, buzzing with the anticipation of the day ahead, our very own Elysian field to rival Centre Court over the road. The smells of freshly cut grass, frying breakfasts and giant coffee vats wafting through the air. A crowd roar every five minutes as a cork popped somewhere in the line. The first day of Wimbledon, my favourite day of the year, had rolled around again.

IS IT REALLY DARKEST JUST BEFORE DAWN?

Murray had been spotted roaring around Surrey driving a Ferrari, but show was not his business and the humble aspiring champ informed us that he had rapidly traded in his 'poser's car'[lviii]. There was not one single English player in the men's singles in 2010, but a respectable two from Scotland. I had long since stopped dividing England and Britain, but it did feel bleak when, for the first time in 133 years, only one Brit singles player made the second round. The Queen ~~grimaced through / endured~~ watched Murray's match, who bowed like a good lad, and dispatched his opponent like a knight. Rafa

228

was reeling with two five-setters in his first three rounds and a jingoistic fever was in the air as Roger almost went out in the first round, lasted a few more, then did tumble in the quarter-finals to dishy Czech Republican Tomas Berdych.

FRUITCAKE

On the second Tuesday I met a man in the gents' toilets who was dressed as a giant strawberry and struggling with the mechanics of his suit at the urinal. This was a first for me, on many levels. Coming all the way from Venice Beach in Los Angeles, where Jim Morrison wandered and wrote his pseudo-cosmic lyrics, Strawberry Man was just as brilliantly offbeat, a veritable psychedelic space fruit warrior. He had slept out for two whole nights to get his Centre Court tickets, but insisted that he 'didn't sleep in the strawberry'. As if.

NOT A GOLDEN ERA IN EVERY SENSE

The men's game may have been drawing comparisons with the glory days of the late 70s and 80s, but on a fashion level it was a complete non-event. They were all starting to look like basketball players with 'technical fibres' creating fitted, but style-less, kit with no elegance and no personality. The giant, plasticated trainers looked like upside down speedboats and only the sartorially precise Roger Federer could really be excluded from the criticism.

SHALL I COMPARE THEE TO A SUMMER'S DAY?

Following the 'writer in residence' idea, which had been recently employed by Marks & Spencer, Wimbledon sent in a poet whose goal was to write one rhyme a day for the whole fortnight. The chosen rhymer, Matt Harvey, was as proud as punch, and embraced the role, vowing to read the compositions to the fans in The Queue. It was immediately brought to the nation's attention that one of his poems began with the line 'Thwackety wackety singety ping, hittety backety pingety zang'. Mr Harvey, interviewed in *The Guardian*, promptly declared, in anticipation of the inevitable poetical snob-lash, 'Look, this is just for pleasure.[62] You're not getting Carol Ann Duffy here, you're just getting me.' It was a good point and I decided immediately that he was a great addition.

THE THEATRE OF TENNIS

Tennis, or sport in general, dove headlong into The Twilight Zone when cheery American John Isner and introspective Frenchman Nicolas Mahut served up a surreal slice of sporting lunacy. The two medium-ranked pugilists met in the first round and proceeded to slug out the longest tennis match, or tragicomedy, in history, lasting three whole days. To put it in perspective it was not just the longest match, it

---

62 He didn't specify whose pleasure, presumably his own.

smashed all records completely, with the last set alone longer than the previous longest <u>entire match</u>. It finished 6-4, 3-6, 6-7, 7-6, 70-68 to John Isner, ending one of the most bizarre and freakish sporting spectacles ever seen.

The two men stumbled around the court in a slightly absurd, almost comical, version of Samuel Beckett's *Waiting for Godot* as they locked horns in an increasingly ~~pointless~~ point-full battle, knowing that whoever won would not recover in time for the next round.

The theatrical hot ticket was presided over by the umpire, Mohamed Lahyani, the only person in the known universe who could break their infernal deadlock and declare a winner. By the end it became less about winning and losing and more about something else altogether. Maybe it was about the power of sport in a pure, gladiatorial form? Maybe it proved how much these international stars actually cared? Maybe everyone had stopped thinking about it and were just waiting for *The One Show* to start. After his 183-game first round in which he served 112 aces, Isner lasted just 23 games in defeat in the second, in which he didn't serve a single one.

'BLESSED IS THE MAN WHO EXPECTS NOTHING, FOR HE SHALL NEVER BE DISAPPOINTED'[lix]

Murray cruised through the early rounds saying he was loving the pressure, and when he saw off Muhammad Ali lookalike Jo-Wilfried Tsonga it was all 'HURRAY FOR MURRAY FROM SURREY'[lx] for the <u>Brit</u> hero. When he went down to Rafa in a Henmanian anti-climax of a semi-final it was 'BETTER LOCH NEXT YEAR' for the Scot[lxi]. I saw hope in the fact that a frustrated Murray was dismissive of the achievement of reaching a semi, adding that even a 'final is not enough', and that he was 'here to win'.

Rafa went on to win his second Wimbledon, beating Berdych in the final. Shortly afterwards, Murray went to Canada and beat Rafa and Roger to win the Open, making you think that, despite his protestations, expectation at SW19 might be weighing a bit heavy on his shoulders. If you looked at the winners of the Australian and French Opens you could certainly observe a distinct lack of home-grown trophy-lifters in recent years, for both men and women, where expectation appeared to crush talents who were playing more freely in other tournaments. The US Open was an exception, but then the Americans of the 70s, 80s and 90s were so good that they pretty much won anywhere they played.

Ladies' Champion *Serena Williams*
Gentlemen's Champion *Rafael Nadal*

WHEN IN WOMBLEDON, DO AS WOMBLES DO ...

The Wombles are a group of furry creatures who recycle rubbish in creative ways and live in burrows. They were created in the 60s by the writer Elizabeth Beresford and went on to become stars of a stop-motion classic TV show and have an astonishingly successful career as pop stars. There are Wombles in every country of the world but the ones we know and love live on Wimbledon Common. Here are ten key facts ...

1. Wombles are scared of humans, and that's the only reason why you never see them.

2. The song 'Wombling Merry Christmas' reached number two on 4 January 1975 – it was only kept off the coveted number one spot by Mud's morose classic, 'Lonely This Christmas'.

3. The term 'Womble' was used for new recruits in the London Fire Brigade during the 70s. Unclear whether it was complimentary or not.

4. Their recycling and environmental concerns were years ahead of their time, making the gang prototype Crusties, just without the tie-dye trousers, dreadlocks, joss sticks and Levellers t-shirts.

5. All of the characters were named after places e.g. Great Uncle Bulgaria, Tobermory and Orinoco.

6. Aside from these furry friends Wimbledon Common was also home to legendary music impresario Don Arden, famed manager of The Small Faces and Black

Sabbath. Legend has it that when Lou Reed stayed with Arden here during the recording of his *Transformer* album, he couldn't understand how the road running by the Common had cluttered all the big houses on one side and none on the other side where the woods began. He came to refer to that side of the road as the 'wild side', becoming the original idea for a song called 'Walk On The Wild Side'.

7. Tomsk is the only Womble who doesn't wear a hat.

8. Bernard Cribbins, of *Fawlty Towers* and *Jackanory* fame, narrated the cartoon in his wonderfully cuddly and comforting voice.

9. The stop-mo show was created by Ivor Wood, an Anglo-French genius who studied fine art and then created *Le Manège Enchanté*, or *The Magic Roundabout*, as we know it. The Elvis of Stop-Mo followed that up with more classics, including *Simon in the Land of Chalk Drawings*, *Paddington* and *The Wombles*, before *Postman Pat* and *Bertha*.

10. The Wombles are, along with The Beastie Boys, the only seriously cool people to play golf.

BONNIE PRINCE ANDY?

American comic Mitch Hedberg once said, 'The depressing thing about tennis is that no matter how good I get, I'll never be as good as a wall.' At January's Australian Open, Murray lost a worryingly one-sided final to a born-again Novak, who was starting to play very much like an extremely agile wall. Djokovic's newly discovered belief reminded you of one of those people who wakes up from a coma and discovers that they can now speak fluent Mandarin. In this case he had suddenly realised that he could be just as good as anyone else, and maybe even better, when it came to winning Majors.

All the pressure on Murray was certainly starting to affect me, especially as Tim never put us through this, the whole 'getting to the final' thing. In the spring Murray reached, and then got beaten by Rafa in, a French Open semi (no shame there), but did win Queen's again. I started to think that maybe he was just 'excellent', in an era when everyone else was 'exceptional'.

ONCE UPON A TIME
In the Lawn Tennis Museum they were holding an exhibition dedicated to The Queue with boards telling the story through the years. This included vintage photographs of gentlemen trying to look dignified in temperatures in excess of a hundred degrees, as they slumped against fences in thick tweed three-piece suits, bowler hats and knee-length socks. Like a modernist art installation, it also featured a Union Jack tent placed in the middle of the space as well as other odd items, including a quasi-religious crown made of tennis balls, as worn by some crazed fan, an actual bag size measurement frame from the security gates and a used tube of Pringles.

FANCY DRESS
Bethanie Mattek-Sands took her weird vestments to a new level when she turned up on court wearing black war paint under her eyes and sporting a white-tassled cowboy jacket covered in spray-painted white tennis balls, which had been carefully sliced in half. Under the coat she wore a white dress with only one sleeve and topped it all off with knee-length football socks. The outfit had supposedly been conceived by ~~a five-year-old~~ one of Lady Gaga's designers, prompting the newspapers to nickname her, somewhat lazily, 'The Lady Gaga of Tennis'. She didn't enjoy Gaga's crossover success, losing in the first round.

Laura Robson rushed in to an early lead against another clothes horse, Sharapova, and then, well, you know. Still, Maria scratched her bum so the papers could all dust off the Athena 'Tennis Girl' images en masse as she went all the way to the final, losing to Petra Kvitova. In other fashion news, the ever-classy Venus stole the true sartorial accolades with an elegant lacy white jumpsuit, which perfectly matched her graceful game.

THE QUEUE ROCKS

My wife's first experience of The Queue was a mixed bag. Arriving at 4.30am the skies drizzled incessantly before dropping some full-on biblical rain at about seven, leaving us both decidedly cheesed off and me harbouring a strange desire to apologise to all the foreign folk who had had their British suspicions confirmed by the inclement weather. On the plus side we met a Danish couple who were the first proper heavy metal rock fans I had ever seen at Wimbledon. We cracked open the Champagne with them at 8.30 in the morning, as they shared one of the most interesting tennis conversations I had ever had, relaying the story of 'Torben Ulrich'. Torben was a Danish top 100 pro tennis player who reached the fourth round at Wimbledon in 1959, but was also a musician, painter, actor, director and writer for jazz aficionado magazines. His son, a gifted junior tennis player called Lars, moved with the family to Los Angeles in 1980, with a plan to hit the big time in the tennis boom period. Lars quickly tired of pounding forehands, starting to pound the drums instead, then launching a band, which he named 'Metallica'. More than 100 million albums later he's probably ok with that decision.

Later on we all watched with Champagne-fuelled amusement as a man from New York tried indiscreetly to tip an Honorary Steward for giving him some information about how long the wait was likely to be. You really don't tip an HS, they are like high-end butlers, like Sir John Gielgud in *Arthur*, and he looked suitably appalled by the idea.

PLUS ÇA CHANGE

You couldn't make this up; Isner and Mahut were just about to unveil the plaque the Club had installed by Court 13 to celebrate last year's epic when they were astonishingly drawn together again in the first round. This time Isner went through unfussily in straight sets, back in the shower nine hours, and two and a half days, earlier than the previous year. Living up to national stereotypes with aplomb, the smiley American, Isner, said the two were now 'really good friends' and the shoe-gazing Frenchman, Mahut, said he had suffered a deep 'depression' the previous year.

LADIES AND GENTLEMEN, ROGER HAS LEFT THE BUILDING

In The Queue, I experienced the full intensity of the Female Federer Fan. Like a cult, called Rogerology, He was treated as a Ruling Overlord of the Galactic Tennis Confederacy, and all the members had been ReRogrammed in a Basel laboratory to believe that anyone in his half of the draw was an inconvenience to be Removed.

The four women next to me on the first Wednesday were a mixture of nationalities, but all slept in a red tent emblazoned with a large Swiss (i.e. 'Roger') flag. They had cut out their own large 'RF' logo and glued it with Copydex on to the canvas on the other side. The Swiss flag made it look so much like a First Aid tent that at one point a sobbing kid with a crew cut stood there banging on the side as he'd cut his knee open on the gravel. The artisanal, hand-made approach was continued in their own attire, with one sporting a red t-shirt proudly displaying what looked like a grinning Jimmy Carr, but turned out to be Roger in half-light. They all, especially the two Irish ladies, 'disapproved of' Andy Murray and would tell anyone that they were 'only here for Roger'.

The gang all saw something unique the next week, in that no one had ever seen King Roger lose from two sets up, because it had never happened before at a Major.

But out he went in the quarters once again, after leading comfortably against Jo-Wilfried Tsonga. He looked entirely unconcerned.

A CHIRPY BUNCH

Twitter was now in full flow, with down-time rich tennis stars embracing its simple distraction. Man of the people, Rafa, even posted a picture of himself in the vegetable aisle at ASDA down the road, displaying an endearing habit of him doing his own shopping whilst out on tour. Andy Murray's Mum, Judy, distracted attention from her son by engaging in some playful Twitter banter with dashingly good-looking Spanish matador, @feliciano_lopez, before Andy called time after she tweeted, 'Ooooooooooh Deliciano … looking good out there. As always.' Particularly as he was playing him in the next round.

LIKE DÉJÀ-VU … ALL OVER AGAIN

They showed the semi-final match between Nadal and Murray on the giant screens on the new No.2 court (the hill was so packed that it was one-on-one-out), with the sound turned off. This new stadium was a personal favourite, sunken in to the ground and hidden away in the ivy-clad south-eastern tip of The Grounds. It was the perfect modern court, with just the right nod to the traditions of the past, but all the best bits of modern comfort and design. Despite all this, watching the semi there still felt a bit like going to Wembley Arena to watch a small screen in one corner, with almost no sound, showing the action going on at Wembley Stadium over the road.

Despite tearing into Rafa for an hour and a half, the semis once again proved Andy's limit. The easiest of forehands when he was a set, and almost another break, up was blazed long and the crowd's aching sense of 'opportunity missed' transferred to his racket as he was broken in the next game, lost his cool, and then the match. The bloke next to me shouted, 'Come on, Murray, put it away, it's not rocket science.' I was so aggrieved that I retorted, 'It may not be "rocket science", but it's still really bloody hard to beat Rafa.' I was so irritated that I felt the need to point out that not everything that isn't 'rocket science' is easy. I think he then insulted me quite aggressively. It was getting to us all.

Afterwards Murray said, in his candid and self-effacing way, 'It's not a valid excuse as a sportsman that you were under pressure,' but when you looked at the astonishing coverage in press, online and in the country as a whole I wasn't 100 per cent convinced that I believed him, imagining how much easier it would be to play without 60 million people watching you through their fingers.

'Tipsy' refers to a much-loved state of revelry, epitomising the merriment just past light-headedness, and before getting blotto, and it is one I often enjoy on a lazy Wimbledon afternoon. On that bleak July evening in 2011 I decided for one of the only times in my life to get drunk at the tennis, as a coping mechanism. The docile, almost accepting manner of everyone's reaction to the defeat made me despondent, the overall feeling making me think of the Thoreau quote about how 'the mass of men lead lives of quiet desperation'. This was me right now. Staring up at the roof of Centre Court, high/ low on Stella Artois, I thought …

This is never going to happen for a British bloke.

This experience is less 'A Handful of Summers', Forbesy, and more a 'Clenched fist punched through a paper wall of summer dreams'.

It's exactly like England not winning a major football tournament. We just don't have that mentality. We think about it too much.

It's like football's '30 years of hurt', but Fred Perry and 70 years.

We're too self-reflective, we're self-absorbed.

We care so much what everyone else thinks of us.

We love the 'it might have been', it's the sad words of John Greenleaf Whittier.

But maybe you can't have it all?

We've got The Beatles <u>and</u> The Stones.

How many great Spanish music groups are there? The Gipsy Kings? I don't even think they're Spanish. They're gipsies.

But sitting there, right then, I'd have swapped The Beatles for a male Wimbledon singles champion. I actually would.

And I <u>really</u> love The Beatles.

The world discussed whether he was just unlucky being born in to this era of tennis which, with Djokovic continuing his astonishing resurrection, was starting to look worryingly like a Big Three, and then Andy. If The Big Four were The Beatles then Raf & Rog were obviously John & Paul, dark horse Novak was George, but did that make Andy Ringo? Was Wimbledon his 'Octopus's Garden?' I kept coming back to the Infinite Monkey Theorem, about how a room of monkeys hitting typewriter keys at random will, given an infinite amount of time, surely type the Complete Works of Shakespeare. By that measure, at some point, after all this time, a British monkey will put together the right combination of forehands, backhands and serves and volleys to just … get … over … the … line. But is Andy that monkey?

Ladies' Champion *Petra Kvitova*
Gentlemen's Champion *Novak Djokovic*

WORK ... IN PROGRESS

The year started with the sensational news that Ivan Lendl was to be Murray's new coach/mentor/cornerman, creating a kind of 'Fire & Ice' combination, and exactly what Murray needed. Icy Lendl was known for having fluffed a fair few finals himself before getting over that crucial 'Major line', and he was also known for being an intensely focused winner, with a keen sense of humour. He displayed this in one post-match interview in the 80s when a correspondent asked him what he considered to be 'the most important point in a match?' A completely deadpan Lendl stared blankly at the reporter before replying, 'The last one.' Defeat in a five-hour classic of a semi-final at the hands of Novak in the Australian Open in January even felt like a step in the right direction for the increasingly impassioned Murray.

'You know what the name Lendl means to me? Dedication, hard work, overcoming everybody although he maybe didn't have the tennis talent of a lot of guys. I admire him immensely.'

Pete Sampras, 1994

HONEYDOOM

After 23 attempts, I was finally the recipient of tickets in the celebrated ballot … in only the second year of my life that I wouldn't set foot in SW19 throughout June and July. This was due to the dates of my own wedding in France and the fact that I was then away on honeymoon for the whole of Wimbledon. It was foolish, and even a signed card from Boris Becker on request from my best man couldn't make up for it. I watched from afar, genuinely praying for Andy, but sort of not wanting to be on a beach when 76 years of real hurt might come to an end. When the news came through that Rafa had gone out to world No.100 Rosol in the second round I actually shivered with excitement/anticipation/fear.

WHAT'S IN A NAME?

In the post-Henman/early-Murray era the 'debate' (excuse for Sue Barker to talk about something at the start of a show) was focused around whether 'The Hill', or 'Henman Hill', where people watched the action on a big screen, should have its name changed to 'Murray Mound'. It was clearly a non-debate as it wasn't really 'called' that anyway; it wasn't like a tube station, or even a road, with a sign, it was just a thing that people said. In the ensuing years, and with each celebrated win, there would be discussions around 'Murray Mount', 'Murray Mountain' and 'Murrayfield', which is in Edinburgh, not even close to where Murray is from, near Glasgow. Incredibly, at one point, there had even been talk of 'Rusedski Ridge' and we reached a nadir as a nation this year as 'Heather Hill' was suggested after Ms Watson reached the third round[63].

---

63 In fact, a new nadir would be reached in 2013 when Laura Robson reached the fourth round and there were 'calls' for 'Robson Green'.

EMOTIONS LAID BARE

I watched the semi-final in the restaurant-bar of a St Tropez naturist beach, which was my only option, as the rest of the beach establishments seemed indifferent to the fact that Andy Murray's opponent, Jo-Wilfried Tsonga, was both French and extremely likeable. They chose instead to show re-runs of *Loft Story* – the French version of *Big Brother,* in which irritating people sit around eating Nutella sandwiches and talking about their feelings. A crosscourt winner two hours later saw Murray take the set, and the match. I could only stand, open-mouthed and surrounded by very naked French people, and gawp. At the screen. Andy was in the Wimbledon final, the first British man since Bunny Austin in 1938. Waiting for him there, somewhat inconveniently, would be tennis's own Chairman of the Board.

Deciding that these *liberté*-loving naturists were a lucky charm I went back two days later when, despite winning his first set in any Major final, and looking like he might have what it took, the rain came down, the roof closed and Federer, the indoor king, closed it out for an incredible seventh title. It was hard to tell from the French TV coverage, the noise of food cooking and the distraction of a constant stream of private parts moving past the screen, but I was pretty sure that the majority of the crowd in the stadium were rooting for Roger. I know that in tennis they are playing for themselves more than their countries, but this still left me feeling disappointed.

Andy cried, 17.3 million watching in Britain cried, I cried, even some of the naturists cried, but that might have been the spitting merguez sausages on the barbecue by the bar. Sue Barker pushed him to express and, clearly on the emotional brink, he just said, 'I'm getting closer.' He gathered himself and said, 'Right, I'm going to try this and it's not going to

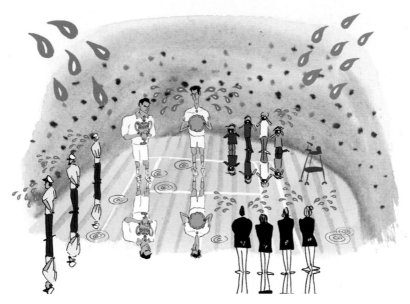

be easy ...' Murray thanked his team, his box, and then had a moment of clarity, gesturing to the crowd, 'And last of all to you guys. Everybody always talks about the pressure of playing at Wimbledon, how tough it is, but it's not the people watching, they make it so much easier to play. The support has been incredible, so thank you.' Andy's girlfriend, Kim, was in tears, I was in tears and even Federer, an old softie at heart, hugged him and looked as though he was in tears himself.

It didn't escape me that this almost joyful, nation-as-one defeat, combined with a slight element of bad luck, with a dash of 'defeat to the better man', especially as it was Jolly Nice Roger, might have been a perfect outcome for some in Middle England. Most, in fact. In all honesty we like losers in Britain. We especially like losers who try really hard, the harder they try and the closer they get, the better. We can leave all that winning to those foreign sorts.

I also felt that the crushing tension of hope and expectation seemed to be pushing Andy in to the ground and, despite these heartfelt words to the contrary, it was starting to feel like he wasn't going to quite get there.

THE GOLDEN RINGS

I got back in time for the Olympics, lucky enough to get some tickets to see Murray storm through his quarter-final, to the backdrop of a country properly tipsy on the sporting spirit. It was bizarre walking around a half-empty All England Club, with Olympic mauve splashed everywhere and giant cut-outs of Wenlock and Mandeville, the one-eyed phallic mascots, staring down at you like surveillance cameras from an ominous dystopian future. Murray lost only one set on the way to the final, beating Djokovic in the semi, and he was rewarded with a reunion for the gold medal match. His old friend, the No.1 seed, Roger, awaited, having never won the Olympics, the only honour missing from his extensive one hundred and forty metre long Swiss Beech trophy cabinet, overlooking Lake Geneva[64].

YOU AGAIN?

Despite my personal frustrations one had to acknowledge how far Federer had brought tennis – a new rarefied air of mass popularity and appreciation of its very finest arts. One of the great joys of watching him, whether you were a Fortnight Fan or an all-yearer, was the incredible tempo of his game. It was almost as if his all-round genius were not enough; he also seemed to understand what the crowd wanted to see, and also how they want to see it. Unlike Rafa, who plays to win by any means necessary and however long that might take, you got the impression with Federer that he would rather lose than drag it out too much, constantly taking half the time of other players between points, playing

---

64 I would imagine.

so fast that it could feel like you were watching the sped-up highlights on TV.

On that sun-baked August day, our have-a-go hero Andy decided that it was his turn to call the shots and dictate the pace. Just four short weeks to the day since the teary final, the boxing fan Murray waded into Federer with a controlled, yet fierce, aggression. The disciplined power was punctuated by a series of crushing right hooks, smashing his rival to smithereens, 6-2, 6-1, 6-4, which Murray immediately hailed as 'the biggest win of my life'. He had never been so dominant or so forceful, a point not lost on Federer, who had 'helpfully' suggested these improvements to Murray before[lxii].

As he stood in triumph, draped proudly in that Union Jack, with Federer looking on slightly longingly for once, it felt like a great big tipping point. Up until then the Union Jack to me was bunting, it was quaint Royal Weddings and street parties, it was Martin Parr taking the piss, it was Tim Henman not quite winning, it was Greg Rusedski and his bandana. It felt ironic and small and made tennis look silly, misguided and middle-class. But now we had someone who was a real, bona fide champion, a genuine victor to be proud of with a bellowing primal roar. Everything changed.

HE'S KING OF THE HILL, TOP OF THE HEAP

In the late New York summer, Murray cruised through the draw to get to another Major final, where he would once again meet ... Novak Djokovic. The reborn Serbian had started to look both unbeatable and also slightly unsettling, his demonic stare and terrifying intensity putting you in mind of Robert de Niro in *Taxi Driver*. In one of the longest title matches on record Murray came through 7-6 (12-10), 7-5, 2-6, 3-6, 6-2, becoming the first British man to win the US Open, and a Major in general, since Fred Perry walked off court in New York in 1936, on exactly the same date of 10 September. I sat in my flat, boozy and ecstatic at 4am, my eyes sore from the tears. I was on my own, so drunk and excited that at one point I actually queued for my own toilet in the flat my wife and I share. This was despite knowing that my wife was in bed and no one else was there, mistakenly thinking that it was occupied, before apologising and waiting patiently outside.

Ladies' Champion *Serena Williams*
Gentlemen's Champion *Roger Federer*

AND IN THE END, THE LOVE YOU TAKE IS EQUAL TO THE LOVE YOU MAKE

Still bathing in the Major-winning glory, Murray got to the final of the next one, the Australian Open, losing to Djokovic, after having taken the first set and looking on the way to breaking his duck in Melbourne. The nation held its breath with an eye on Wimbledon as he pulled out of the French with a hip injury, but the papers were soon full of photos of him looking calm and focused on the green, green grass of home, getting ready for his date with destiny. Well, either that or another sickening defeat.

'Champions are not born. They are made. They emerge from a long, hard school of defeat, discouragement, and mediocrity, but they are endowed with a force that transcends discouragement and cries, "I will succeed."'

Bill Tilden

WILLIAMS THE CONQUEROR

The first week kicked off with Maria Sharapova and Serena Williams publicly squabbling over dishy Bulgarian, Grigor

'Baby Fed' Dimitrov. He was given the nickname not because he would scream on court and suck on a dummy, but due to his similar, if junior, style of playing to Federer. Grigor's dashing good looks had apparently been irresistible for both the tennis legends and had resulted in some decidedly un-Wimbledon bickering. The icily Taylor-Swiftian Sharapova could be the master of the withering put-down and Serena, favouring a more direct approach, was hardly backwards in coming forwards, making for a frequently frosty relationship.

While Serena held an incredible record against pretty much all of the active players on the tour[65], she held an embarrassingly one-sided one against Sharapova, which was no doubt a contributing factor. Her faultless pop culture assault accompanied her dominance, with outrageous outfits, her own fashion label, screaming at umpires, holding all four Majors at once, doing totally nuts photo shoots in the altogether and being by far the oldest female No.1 of all time. She summed it up pretty well herself, saying, 'If we all liked the same thing, it would make the world a really boring place! What matters most is that I like myself.' Even Ms Sharapova didn't have anything to say to that.

BOY, YOU'RE GONNA CARRY THAT WEIGHT

On-court expectation was sky-high and fortunately Murray seemed to be revelling in the weight on his shoulders. I had been at Queen's to watch him win his third title and the air around the camp, with a relaxed Lendl very much at the centre, was making everything feel distinctly different. There were no major proclamations from Murray, no 'THIS TIME I'LL DO IT's, but he had a certain air of calm focus and authority about him, and it seemed that a showdown

---

65 Apart from Justine Henin, but she had retired by now, nipping a potentially perfect rivalry in the bud.

with his clear rival for top dog billing, world No.1 Novak Djokovic, was exactly where this was heading.

Murray's first round victim was one 'B. Becker' from Germany, his defeat of the unrelated Benjamin feeling like a particularly good sign to me. When Nadal, fresh from an incredible eighth French Open win, crashed out to No.135 Steve Darcis it looked even more likely. Federer then incredibly followed suit, bowing out to No.116 Sergiy Stakhovsy in a 'stick it up 'em' whirlwind of serve and volley, as the whole country gasped as one.

WE LOVE LAURA

Smiley Laura Robson was nice as ninepence and, after a couple of false starts since her junior title, she was stealing hearts all over the place with her infectious brand of go-get-'em tennis and her girl-next-door charm. The beaming 18-year-old put out the No.10 seed on the way to the fourth round, and only lost there, if you believed the papers, because bad omen David Cameron tweeted her a 'good luck' message. She also won an army of One Direction fans with her cheeky tweets about the band, making the tournament feel pop-y and fun, like the Eighties.

Elsewhere Maria Sharapova and her orange undercrackers were dumped out by the shriektastic Michelle Larcher de Brito. Jonathan Liew, writing in the *Daily Telegraph,* vividly likened them to 'fishwives on the pier at sundown ... fighting a feral contest'. Out-shrieked Maria was none too happy about the slippery surface, echoed elsewhere as a further seven players pulled out on that day alone due to the dangerously lustrous grass.

WELL AND TRULY TOASTED

On the first Thursday I woke up, had some Bovril on toast (a tradition, I did this during the US Open final) and walked down from my flat to queue in the rain at 9am, getting in line for Murray's potentially tricky Friday encounter with the resurgent Spaniard Tommy Robredo. I harboured a genuine belief that my presence was crucial at this match, on some kind of supernatural level. It had come to that. My colleague at work asked why I didn't just text my old friend Matt Little and ask him to set me aside some tickets. I explained that this was not exactly how it worked at elite level sport, how a professional sportsman aiming to break 77 years of history would probably be working with a strength and conditioning coach who remained focused on the strength and conditioining bit of that goal, as opposed to worrying about sorting tickets for people he used to play with at a church tennis club 23 years previously. Just a hunch.

On arrival I was staggered when handed a Queue card showing 'No.508', which was nothing short of a catastrophe, Ranjani Iyer Mohanty's FIFO rule in horrifying effect. The Club allocate 500 tickets to Centre Court, where Murray would almost definitely be playing, and 500 to each of the other three showcourts, normally meaning that some of the 507 people in front of me would go and watch someone else, as there will always be fans of particular players, or nationalities who were not as obsessed by the 77-year wait for a British male champion as us. But the weather was deteriorating and with Centre being the only court with a roof, I drew the assumption that every single person planning on Queuing for 36 hours would request tickets for that court. And I would miss out by eight people, or about three minutes. Or a slice of Bovril on toast.

LONELINESS BREEDS IN LARGE GROUPS OF PEOPLE

The rain continued to pour down in the late afternoon, as I stared despondently from my soggy tent amidst the huge crowd of fellow waiters. On one side three women from Worcester had made a sign and stuck it on the outside of the tent, one half saying 'KEEP CALM AND WATCH THE TENNIS' and the other, 'TENNIS … WITH A CHANCE OF DRINKING'. To the other side were eight Scottish lads, graduates, who had headed down that day from Edinburgh, drank freely and annoyed pretty much everyone, in part as they did not look at all bothered by the weather. And because they were shouting a lot.

At about 9pm I got a knock on my tent. The grads next door were heading into Wimbledon village 'for a few' and wanted to ask if I would mind keeping an eye on their tents. I told them that I couldn't care less personally, but if the stewards got wind of it they'd be out, advice they completely ignored.

THE LUCK OF THE SCOTTISH

At 6am when I awoke I noticed that there was no one in the play tent next to me. The bloke opposite peered out of his door at the drizzly scene and said, 'I think they should bring forward plans to put a roof on The Queue.' An hour later we were all instructed to pack up our belongings and the stewards came over to find out where the boozy academics had got to. I could see a chink of light in the gloom of the wet park.

Half an hour later a shapeless mass of noise staggered across the field, laughing their heads off and still clutching cans of Stella. The cheery hedonists informed me beerily that they were going to skip the tennis that day as they hadn't been to bed and promptly dragged their tent straight over to The Queue for Saturday. I instantly jumped eight people in The Queue. 508 minus 8 = 500. I was in.

'The fight is won or lost far away from witnesses – behind the lines, in the gym and out there on the road, long before I dance under those lights.'

Muhammad Ali

PHYSICAL CHESS

Under the roof on Friday Murray was imperious, dispatching stolid Robredo in his most scintillating form and looking every-inch the player to fear in the men's draw. The atmosphere was super-charged, the closed roof on the old arena making it feel like a film set for a gladiator movie, the packed stands lapping up every moment of Murray's strategically brilliant tennis and his perfectly timed assaults on the ball.

Youzhny followed in the fourth round leading to a not-as-straightforward-as-it-looked quarter-final against unseeded Fernando Verdasco on the Wednesday evening tea-time slot, by which time the country was bathed in warm summer sun.

WE'RE GOING TO NEED SOME FERGIE TIME

Murray had struggled with Fernando, the glamour boy of Spanish tennis, before and when he lost the first two sets in what seemed like no time, 'That Henman Feeling' washed over the entire country like a tidal wave. I was supposed to be at a work event, but I was standing in a pub in Soho, with my back facing the screen, unable to watch the horror unfolding. Other people chatted away, half-watching, eating Twiglets, ironically putting Duran Duran songs on the jukebox ... how I envied them. How could they not feel the tension? Oh, to not care!

But Murray dug deep, feeding off the crowd in a way no other Brit ever had before, seeming to use their fear as a weapon, turning the tension in his favour. He was playing horribly, but it didn't matter – he was clinging on.

The cameras constantly turned to his watching fretful mother but also, significantly, to Sir Alex Ferguson, in a seat nearby. The former Manchester United manager, that master of the comeback, the greatest drinker in the last-chance saloon, was willing his countryman on, his presence making me feel more positive. Fergie <u>always</u> won in the end. Sure enough Murray dug deep, turning it round in five white-knuckle sets for a place in a semi-final which had looked well beyond his grasp. In the wise words of Martina Navratilova, 'What matters isn't how well you play when you're playing well. What matters is how well you play when you're playing badly.'

The semi-final was utterly winnable, even if Murray was playing someone who had beaten him within the last year and was also a doppelgänger for a young Ivan Lendl. At 6ft 8in Jerzy Janowicz of Poland had been nicknamed 'LANKENSTEIN'[lxiii] and his Ivanisevic-like (or Ivanisevic-lite) big serve and slightly cuckoo personality meant anything could happen. It almost did, before Murray found his feet and closed it out under the roof as the rains came down. Here we go, again.

THAT'S WHAT FRIENDS ARE FOR

Everyone's second favourite player, the lugubrious Argentinian Juan Martin Del Potro, was a former sparring partner of Murray's and whilst they had a bit of 'previous' off the court, the relationship had grown and they now appeared to be firm friends. When 'DelPo' won the US Open in 2009, astonishingly clawing his way back to beat the then-virtually unbeatable Federer in the final, the world was his oyster, but injuries had taken their toll and he was only now working his way back up the rankings.

The four hour 43 minute semi-final between him and Novak Djokovic was about as good as it gets, with rallies straight out of a 'Best Of Wimbledon' video and DelPo, the absolute clear 'cool kid in the class', milking the crowd's love for all it was worth. When he found himself on Novak's side of the net after one lungbuster of a rally he playfully zipped up the front of Djokovic's shirt, and you couldn't help feel, in his sporting reaction, that even Novak was enjoying this particular ride. After the longest-ever semi, I was hoping that even the super-human Serbian was slightly depleted.

THIS IS IT … ISN'T IT?

The country now sweltered in a heatwave and the crowds in Wimbledon village were gathered an hour before the pubs opened as, fittingly, we had to queue just to get in to the Rose & Crown. I was worried by some papers' focus on Novak's repeated visits to the Buddhapadipa Temple by the Common, what with all its Zen powers and focus on serenity, and couldn't help but feel that this merry madness around Murray must be benefiting his foe. The BBC showed footage of the two players' Mums having a glass of Champagne together beforehand and their bonhomie made me feel strangely more nervous. I took my seat in the pub, surrounded by friends and family, lost in my own private anguish, as once again (as in all his finals) he was up against the best player in the world; the unstoppable rubber wall of attrition that was Novak Djokovic.

ACT ONE

The first set saw Murray nick a break at 3-3 and close it out comfortably, 6-4. The early lead served only to make me more nervous; as an England football fan I had experienced similar false dawns, seeing us score first in a World Cup quarter-final I knew we'd go on to lose. I remember not caring that I wasn't there in the stadium, but just being thrilled that there were about 300 people in the pub, watching on the various big screens they had put up, vociferously providing that sense of a collective pull, of a shared experience, however painful it might be.

ACT TWO

The second set started in the worst possible way as an early break, and Novak serving first, meant Murray was soon 4-1 down. But it still felt different, almost other-worldly. Or maybe it was the fourth pint of Kronenbourg. Murray's head didn't drop and he looked strangely in control, despite the scoreline. Hemingway defined courage as 'grace under pressure', and that was what we were witnessing as Murray seemed unflustered, almost serene, regrouping and playing like a man possessed to take six of the next seven games and, incredibly, the second set, 7-5. The whole beer garden stood up and roared as one, the giant screens showing Murray walking calmly to his chair.

ACT THREE

The third set was completely dreamlike, even just the fact that he was two sets to love up in the Wimbledon final. I was only too aware of the fact that Novak loved a mountain to climb, and two sets up meant nothing to him – if anything he was even more dangerous.

Federer had all too frequently stood on the brink against the Serbian rubber band man before finding himself on the losing side an hour later. My subconscious was drifting off somewhere else entirely and it wasn't helped when Tim Henman, in the commentary box with Boris, decided to go 'off-script'. At a change of ends the camera drifted over the boating lake in the park where swans were gliding, leading Henman to ponder, 'Have you ever met anyone who's had their arm broken by a swan?' Even Boris was stumped by that one.

Murray broke early in the third and, despite some of the tensest points I had ever known, he held on to serve for the title at 5-4. 'He can smell the roses, but he's still a long way from them,' said Becker, as if inviting us all into a hallucinogenic Borisian dream. That last game will never leave me, like 30 years of my life condensed into one 20-minute spell, and I can see the points playing out now.

Decent serve, Novak goes long with a backhand.

'15-0.'

Brilliant rally and a short Novak drop shot is put away emphatically. The crowd erupts, this is really happening.

'30-0.'

Decent serve, Djokovic goes long! OH. MY. GOD.

'40-0.'

Three Championship points. 'Quiet please.' Murray pauses when about to serve. Someone pops a Champagne cork in the pub and cheers burst out of every corner. Someone tries to shake my hand as if it is over, which irritates me intensely. Andy looks nervous. Kim clutching her hands together. A strong serve but Novak recovers and puts away an easy volley. Still two more.

'40-15.'

Really long first serve, then Novak swats away a short second.

'40-30.'

Oh no. Only one left. Serve looks long and, despite a slightly futile Murray challenge, it's shown as almost a foot out.

Djokovic is grinning. I feel sick, how is Murray even holding a racket? Second serve, a rally, Murray goes long. Oh God. I feel like my nerves made that go out.

'Deuce.'

Murray nets an easy forehand. The crowd groan. Judy stands up and claps him on. I keep thinking it looks like the kind of footage they show in the *Worst Ever Sporting Chokes* DVD, of which I am sure this is going to be the integral part.

'Advantage Djokovic.'

Andy looks exhausted, exasperated, almost too calm. Like he knows his awful fate. More grinning from Djokovic. In the immortal words of BBC Radio's Jonathan Overend, 'He looks like a Bond villain … if he had a cat he'd be stroking it.'[66] Lendl unmoved, staring ahead. Great first serve, Djokovic goes long.

'Deuce.'

A great rally, Novak comes to net, clips net with half volley and it dribbles over.

'Advantage Djokovic.'

How did this happen? From 40-0. I know, I absolutely know, that Murray must win this game. He will not recover from having had, and lost, three Championship points. Nothingy first serve hits the tape, looping second and we're in to a long rally. Brave Andy, painting the lines, hitting deeper, braver,

---

66 Overend said afterwards, 'I've never seen a match of that significance where the person so far behind was so close to victory. The closest Djokovic came to victory was when he was match-point down. You could see it in his eyes. Our box is in the corner of the court, and after one point in that last game he walked down to get his towel right in front of us. He turned to the spectators and smirked. It was as if he was saying, "I'm in business here and you lot will still be in your seats in 2½ hours' time."'

scrapes the baseline before unleashing a crushing forehand winner from a short Novak forehand.

'Deuce'!!!

Murray looks calm again. I actually think I am going to be sick. Big serve, exchange and then an audacious drop shot from Murray, which would beat anyone else on the tour. Not Novak. He goes crosscourt and the sinking feeling is back.

'Advantage Djokovic.'

Murray slightly shakes his head. Big serve, astonishing guts from Murray who thumps a forehand and sets up an easy volley, followed by the most convincing fist pump I have ever seen. He's not going anywhere, I can feel it. It's …

'Deuce'!!

Serve into the net, but it doesn't matter, we're into a Novak-controlled rally, Andy hitting shorter and shorter, Novak in for a simple overhead, his weak spot, but plays it safe, Murray attacks, Novak with defensive volley, chased down by Murray and boom! Novak can only dribble it in to the net. Another Championship point!

'Advantage Murray.'

I know this is it. The first serve's solid, the crowd cheers as if Novak's gone long, it lands on the line, Murray solid … Novak winds up his backhand and fires it into the net … It all goes white, a brilliant white light.

The last thing I remember seeing, somewhat pointedly, was Andy hugging my old tennis club pal Matt Little and then an almost tearful Ivan Lendl. This giant of the game, who shaped its modern form, coaching a fiercely determined man to the title he was unable to win himself, and breaking

a 77-year British curse. The pub had become a riot of noise and spray, people were throwing drinks all over the place, someone was on my shoulders, strangers hugging each other, I think I was crying. I can't believe what has just happened.

Am I dreaming?

'There hasn't been a British Wimbledon men's champion since me in 1936, and a lot of people keep wondering when we will produce another one. Well, it's not a matter of producing anybody, to begin with. It's a case of somebody, somewhere, who wants to succeed badly enough and is determined and bloody-minded enough to make sure he does.'

Fred Perry, 1984

Ladies' Champion *Marion Bartoli*
Gentlemen's Champion *Andy Murray*

EPILOGUE
– 2016 –
LIKE BUSES

JUNE

I decided to end my semi-professional queuing career in 2013 – hitting 40 made it seem about right. The albatross had been lifted emphatically from our national necks, the trophy had been lifted on that sweltering Sunday afternoon and, as my Grandad always told me, 'Don't try and reheat a soufflé.'

One June evening in 2016, I found myself in our garage, looking for a book. My trusty one-man tent was hanging on the wall, next to the box helpfully marked 'Christmas' and another, less helpfully, marked 'Box of Things'. There was an old green Wimbledon bag containing a torch, a sleeping bag, a freebie rug from the *Daily Telegraph*, a flask and some earplugs. It felt nostalgic, like the opening to *The Snowman*[67] when they showed it on Channel 4, as David Bowie rummages through the loft, finding the old blue scarf and suddenly we all realise that he <u>was</u> the boy from the film.

Maybe just one more tilt? Just a really early morning? In truth my queuing days hadn't allowed me to see anything particularly celebrated on a globally significant scale; I had seen a bit of one final (the Martina one when David The Kindly Steward had let us in on the QT for the last set of history-making), no semi-finals and only a couple of quarter-finals. But I had seen some epic battles, nerve-shredding tension, and great courage[68], most often in the first week, when the fear of defeat creates greater frisson and the desire to win can be felt most emphatically. I wouldn't swap those relatively small moments for anything. In more immortal words from my Grandad, life is all about 'the moments between the moments'.

JULY

It's 3am on the first Monday. Packed lunch in the fridge, coffee in a flask, I kiss my sleepy wife and wrap myself in six layers

---

67 Written by Wimbledon native, Raymond Briggs.

68 I use the word courage loosely. It's only a game, after all, not a war. Despite what the papers might have you think.

of warmth and impervious rubber. As I trudge down the hill in the drizzle the back of No.1 Court gracefully rises up from the grey mist. I am stopped in my tracks by an overwhelming feeling of nostalgia and happiness, like eating a spoonful of condensed milk straight from the fridge. I am so incredibly excited by the idea of getting in line that I break into a light jog.

At 4.15am I am handed my Queue card; Number 1,053. The Japanese couple in front of me are fast asleep and a chatty guy from Merseyside behind me is talking to the six girls next to him, who appear not to have been to bed. Despite the fact that it feels like November, I curl up on my rug and manage to doze off. An hour later I am exchanging childhood stories with Neil, my Liverpudlian neighbour, who happens to have been born down the road from my Dad near Bootle, and appreciates my stalker-like knowledge of Liverpool's Beatle sites.

As the clock ticks, the clouds clear and the first ray of sunshine, at about 8.30am, brings the expected cheer from the damp unwashed thousands, huddled together in an unremarkable suburban park, on a Monday morning, as the rest of the world heads off to work. I feel that overwhelming sense of community, of being a part of something, and I wish that some of the players were here to see it. They would be amazed at what people are willing to go through to see them play.

My relatively lowly place in The Queue only gets me a No.2 Court seat, but it's my favourite arena, the order of play looks promising and the weather is getting better by the minute. By the time we reach the free promo coffee stand I am touched to find that the Japanese couple to my left, who have not yet said a word, and seem able to sleep standing up, have returned with a tray of coffees, including cups for both Neil and I. We break the language barrier when I say, 'Nishikori!', and give the big thumbs-up. We work out that they are from

Kyoto and, having visited once before, we cobble together conversation based on a charades version of noodle soup-eating, pretending to marvel at pagodas and big smiles.

Later that day, in a break at the start of the second set of a Nick Kyrgios match, I gaze over across the court to the same row on the other side, where I pick out Neil, laughing about something with the lady next to him. Seeing me, he puts down his flask and waves enthusiastically. I return the compliment. It is strangely uplifting.

On leaving my seat I wander aimlessly around the outside courts, one of the great joys of Wimbledon in the first week, to watch grizzled former Somebodies on the way down dragging their injury-riddled creaking frames into battle with young HopeToBes, all lithe limbs, dreams and untapped energy. As I walk behind Court 10 I bump into my Queue friends from Kyoto. 'Nishikori!!!' they beam, giving a double thumbs-up and eating some more imaginary soup.

Another hour of aimless strolling, like a tennis *flâneur*, a delightful pint of Stella on the hill and I decide to call it a day. It's 8pm, the pleasant summer evening is drawing in and I'm shattered. On the walk back up Victoria Drive to my flat I notice how it feels like days, not 16 hours, since the reverse journey. In front of a small house an old boy is tending his garden. He looks up and smiles, 'Good day at the tennis, son?'

'Not bad. Most of the Brits went out, sun came out in the end.'

'Nothing changes,' he says cheerily, without looking up.

Again, it is strangely uplifting.

LIFE IMITATES CRAP FILMS ART

Brit Marcus Willis looked every bit the Richard Curtis dreamboat with his foppish good looks, slightly goofy sense of humour and world ranking of No.772. He had dragged himself through pre-qualifying, then qualifying and all the way to the main draw. Willis had been in the top 20 juniors in the world ten years before, but had famously been sent home from the Australian Open by the LTA after turning up both late for training and also without his rackets. You could see their point.

In a 'you-couldn't-make-it-up' denouement he beat a player ranked more than 700 places above him to riotous scenes on Court 17, before facing none other than the human GOAT in the second round under the roof on Centre Court. After being understandably overawed in the first set he settled down and started to play a bit, seen particularly with an audacious lob over the seven-time champion, who managed a wry smile as the crowd roared. Willis won a respectable seven games and departed in style, adding, 'I've earned myself a beer, I think.'

LATER

A generally miserable first week of weather led to another Middle Sunday, or 'People's Sunday', as some papers rather patronisingly called it, as if the rest of the time no 'people' are allowed in to Wimbledon. This time the decision was made to do the ticketing entirely online, announced shortly before going cyber-live. Rather than a celebration of tennis the lack of Queue made the process feel like a celebration of tech, and it didn't seem anywhere near as fair to me.

Waiting, queuing, is, like tennis, a meritocracy at Wimbledon. I will proudly stand in line, I will be nice to people, I will suffer the odd Loopy Lou, not gladly, but with relevant tolerance. Round here the early bird catches the showcourt worm. No one wants to get up at 3am, but you do, because you want to get a ticket that much, it's just FIFO. No pain, no gain. Probably a bit of rain.

As I read this 'iQueue' ticketing news I felt, for once, truly part of the movement they called the 'Real Fans', who want it just a bit more, who rally against these things being decided by who's got the best fibre-coaxial internet connection. I still tried and tried, but in the end I didn't get one. I watched impassively on the Sunday, observing a day of relative mediocrity, compared to previous years, and the distinct lack of the euphoria which a delirious, and wildly tired, crowd can bring. It was flat, and that's because people didn't want it enough. Buy with one click, like Nespresso pods on Amazon. com, or want it so bad that you spent the night sleeping in a park? I know who I'd want watching me play. You can't help but feel that the Club would have noticed that as well – they recognise the importance of The Queue and no doubt also notice any dips in atmosphere.

This current Queue set-up in the park will continue for the foresseable future, even if it has something of the temporary feel about it. This is largely because the camping area is on ground all owned by Merton Council and the golf course part is owned by the Club, but leased out until 2043. We will have to wait until then to see a potentially unified Queue experience, all run by the AELTC, which I imagine would be better for everyone. That way it could be embraced fully, like at a Formula One race, or Glastonbury, making the camping an actual, official part of the experience, with the same level of hospitality and services you can get inside.

For guaranteed court preferences on the Middle Saturday you can now spend two whole nights in a tent, which seems a little excessive, even by British standards. This increased demand shows no sign of slowing and we know that the Club would be highly unlikely to abandon a tradition which is both unique to them, and which they know the fans love. They have shown their support for the queuing tradition repeatedly over the last century, a fact seen most recently in the dedicated pamphlet produced, and one imagines that this will continue, even in our increasingly online world. As these 30 years have shown, I am intensely resistant to change when it comes to Wimbledon traditions and That Queue is the pumping, inclusive heartbeat of Wimbledon, the very soul of The Championships, and always has been.

SECOND SUNDAY

I had always harboured a strong desire for Boris Becker to take over the reins with Andy Murray at some point. I just felt like it would be a natural fit. For me, at least. This dream was dashed when Becker started coaching Novak Djokovic, with incredible success, leading to the almost-Brit holding all four Majors coming into the tournament, an unprecedented achievement in the modern era.

The previous Christmas Day I had met Boris for a second time, this one taking place on Wimbledon Common, as he walked with his family and I with mine. We exchanged season's greetings and, as ridiculous as it sounds, I could have sworn he looked at me as if he remembered something. For half a second I was tempted to tell him we had met before, 27 years earlier, just after he had shouted at me.

Novak crashed out early, unsurprisingly struggling for motivation after his all-conquering year, and he was followed by Federer, who went out in the semis. An authoritative Murray cruised through with relative ease and when he beat Berdych to make the final for the third time he would face Federer's conqueror, the genial Canadian giant, Milos Raonic. It was the first time he had faced anyone other than Djokovic or Federer in a Major final. Raonic looked like one of those clean-cut 1950s American ad men, referred to himself as 'the CEO of Milos Raonic tennis', but had a vicious serve and a vastly improved all-round game, helped in part by some grass court coaching from John McEnroe.

With a couple of BBC Sports Personality of the Year awards and a Davis Cup win behind him Murray's popularity

had soared and Ivan Lendl was also back in the Guru/Mentor/
Coach role, having unexpectedly reignited their relationship
in June. Murray had been mostly working with Frenchwoman
Amélie Mauresmo in the intervening period, a pioneering
decision which saw him become the first leading male player
to engage a female coach. He never for a moment looked like
not beating the likeable Canadian and the moment of his
second title felt just as good in repeat, like the bit at the end
of The Beatles' 'Hello Goodbye' when the music stops and
then starts up again in a whirling Hawaiian mass of loveliness.

I was interviewed on the BBC's coverage from the
Rose & Crown, where I did my best (drunk) Kevin Keegan
impersonation by tearily suggesting, as Murray served for the
title, that I would 'love it, really love it' if he won. Most of my
friends saw it, as they repeated it on the news over the next
24 hours, and I also received a Facebook message referencing
it from someone I last saw at a Deacon Blue concert at
Hammersmith Odeon in 1988.

WINNING MENTALITY

Wandering back from the pub I started thinking about the
vast difference between Wimbledon now and when I first
started watching, just over 30 years ago. That first experience
defined Wimbledon for me, as first experiences always do, just
as there must be ten-year-old boys going for the first time now.
Poor souls, they will grow up thinking that there is always a
British bloke in at least the last four. Back in my day there
was a galaxy of international stars and our national obsession
was less about winning it than just getting a couple of people
in to the second week. Tennis was about a two-week period
when we all tuned in to watch the sexy foreign stars with
their tans, great hair and gnarly tempers. But now we had
a contagious new winning form of Britishness which was in
danger of becoming the norm. It might have started with

Jonny Wilkinson and the 2003 Rugby World Cup, it largely sidestepped football, before we had Bradley Wiggins, then the Olympics Success Fest with Jessica Ennis, Mo Farah and all the rest.

But now what? Has it all made any difference? Probably not. We have the biggest tournament in the world and a generation of players who are actually good, but something makes me think that we'll go back to normal service at some point quite soon. The women have served the country better but the 40-year mark will soon be reached without a ladies' champion as well. The bottom line is that for all Wimbledon's wonder and uniqueness, despite its incredible global reputation, the game of tennis is just not part of our national psyche and spirit like football, cricket, rugby and even athletics.

But maybe it doesn't really matter. Who cares what happens now, what comes after, what might be round the corner? We'll always have Wimbledon, we'll always have those two weeks of suspended reality when everyone becomes an expert and there's nothing else on TV and we collectively hope as a nation, get behind something, someone, anyone.

EVERYONE FOR TENNIS

I don't know what Andy Murray's wins actually did for me on a personal level, but I certainly found something in him that I could really relate to. I had grown up loving McEnroe's jerky, slightly unsettling, genius and trying to ape Connors' brutish appeal. Becker's emotional rollercoasting was a ride that caught me at just the right age and I feel lucky to have seen the greatest of them all, Federer, in full flow, and to have observed at first hand the brutal persistence and focus of his nemesis, Nadal. But we'd all waited for Murray and that made him all ours in a very special way. For all of his fierce competitive spirit you always sensed that Murray felt like he was a part of the crowd, of the fans, like he understood what we were all going through and knew that he might just be the man to do something about it. As a player he had a little bit of everything, combining power with touch, as he banished the idea of tennis in this country being all polite, genteel and sissyish. He played tennis like a boxer, stumbling around between points like he was on the ropes, nursing a bloodied nose, swinging wildly before landing one on the chin, getting back on top, then putting his man down in the last round with a knockout forehand.

Murray also had a very peculiar type of grit; that very British, almost Perryian, desire to just Get Over The Line. Even though it would be the more British thing to Almost But Not Quite Get Over The Line. It says everything about our Britishness that Andy had to become a better, more dramatic, more theatrical loser for us to love him – his winning in 2013 to some seemed less interesting than his losing in 2012. I don't care that he wasn't, and won't be, a more successful player than Roger, or Rafa, or Novak, because it was never about that. It was about having someone to really compete at the very top, and every now and then make us proud. And win bloody Wimbledon. The fact that fate chose to give us our best player in almost a century at a time when Spain, Serbia and, especially, Switzerland all had the same idea is just one of those things.

But, most significantly, Andy Murray had an incredible patience. He wasn't afraid of standing in line for his turn. Kipling had it right in 'If', but in this case, Wimbledon might have chosen the wrong line to put above the door. They should have used this.

'If you can wait and not be tired by waiting …'

Come to think of it, that's Wimbledon in a nutshell.

Walter D. Whintle, a poet from the 19th century about whom very little is known, wrote 'Thinking'. It is also known as 'The Man Who Thinks He Can', which I find much preferable.

If you think you are beaten, you are;
If you think you dare not, you don't.
If you'd like to win, but you think you can't,
It is almost a certain – you won't.
If you think you'll lose, you're lost;
For out in this world we find
Success begins with a fellow's will
It's all in the state of mind.
If you think you're outclassed, you are;
You've got to think high to rise.
You've got to be sure of yourself before
You can ever win the prize.
Life's battles don't always go
To the stronger or faster man;
But sooner or later the man who wins
Is the one who thinks he can!

The poem was most likely published in
1905 by Unity Tract Society,
Unity School of Christianity

'Everything I am, everything that I have and everything that I will be, it is because of this court so I have nothing but great memories, I wouldn't change a thing, this place very much became my home.'

Boris Becker [lxiv]

OUTTAKES

There are a lot of chapter title puns in this little tome. But not half as many as there could have been. In the style of the actors' mistakes they used to put at the end of films like *The Cannonball Run*, here are some which didn't make the cut.

1. DON'T, MURRAY! BE HAPPY!
2. ROBSON'S CHOICE
3. GRASS IS FOR COW(ANS)
4. ARMAGEDDON OUT OF HERE
5. STICH IN THE MUD
6. FOR PETE'S SAKE!
7. BRIT-TLE
8. HELL HATH NO FURY LIKE A GREGORY SCORNED
9. WIMBLE-DON-UT
10. NO ATTEMPT TO MURRAY FAVOUR
11. DIAMOND IN THE RAF
12. THE LAND OF RODD
13. A ROG IS A MAN'S BEST FRIEND
14. MAR-TEEN AS MUSTARD
15. A KNIGHT IN SHINING UNDER ARMOUR
16. READY, STEADY, JO
17. A FEDERER IN HIS CAP
18. P.D.QUEUE
19. WIMBLE-PRIMA-DON-A
20. CLIFF, YOU CAN KEEP YOUR HEAD, WHILE THE REST OF US ARE LOSING OURS
21. WIMBLE-DON DRAPER
22. AN ENGLISHMAN'S HOME IS HIS ANDREW CASTLE
23. BEGGARS CAN'T BE QUEUERS
24. BETWEEN YOU, ME AND THE TENT POST
25. CHAMP AT THE BIT
26. YOU CAN'T MURRAY LOVE
27. NOLE VAULT
28. HITTING A GREEN AND PURPLE PATCH
29. MAC AND RUIN
30. RIFF-RAF
31. JIMMY'S RIDDLE
32. SORT THE WHEAT FROM THE RAF
33. WHAT COULD POSSIBLY GO-RAN?
34. WIMBLEDON'T

READ ON

If you enjoyed this light-hearted read then you might be ready to step up a few weights and take on some heavier action. The books below were both an inspiration in writing this one, and also the best, or perhaps 'most enjoyable, books I have read on the subject.

- Wilson, Elizabeth *Love Game* (Serpent's Tail, London 2014)
- Drucker, Joel, *Jimmy Connors Saved My Life* (Robson Books, London 2005)
- Feinstein, John *Hard Courts: Real Life on the Professional Tennis Tours* (Villard Books, New York 1991)
- Adams, Tim *Being John McEnroe (Yellow Jersey, London 2004)*
- Forbes, Gordon *A Handful of Summers* (Heinemann, London 1978)
- Mitchell, Kevin *Break Point* (John Murray, London 2015)
- Smith, Martin, *Anyone For Tennis? The Telegraph Book of Wimbledon* (Bloomsbury, London 1989)
- Bodo, Peter *The Courts of Babylon* (Pocket Books, NYC 1995)
- Ware, Susan *Game, Set, Match: Billie Jean King and the Revolution in Women's Sports* (The University of North Carolina Press, North Carolina 2015)
- Barrett, John *Wimbledon: The Official History* (Vision Sports Publishing, London 2014)
- Ashe, Arthur *Days of Grace* (Ballantine Books, New York 1993)
- Tignor, Stephen *High Strung: Björn Borg, John McEnroe & the Untold Story of Tennis' Fiercest Rivalry* (Harper Collins, New York 2011)
- Harman, Neil *Court Confidential* (The Robson Press, London 2013)
- Evans, Richard *McEnroe: A Rage for Perfection* (Simon & Schuster, New York 1982)
- Henderson, Jon *The Last Champion: The Life of Fred Perry* (Yellow Jersey, London 2010)
- Barnes, Simon *The Meaning of Sport* (Short Books, London 2007)

IN MEMORY OF PETER DOOHAN
1961–2017

'I didn't lose a war. Nobody died. I just lost a tennis match.'

Boris Becker's famously philosophical post-match comments fell on deaf ears to me that day in June 1987, as a young fan of the champion. I would never forget the man who beat him, the Australian Peter Doohan, who was immediately nicknamed 'The Becker Wrecker' by the papers. Looking back, it was undoubtedly the biggest shock in Wimbledon history, not because Doohan was a no-hoper, but because of how invincible Boris appeared to be on the grass of SW19. The 19-year-old had never lost on the storied lawns – he'd withdrawn injured then won it twice – and it made him seem unbeatable.

Doohan hailed from New South Wales on Australia's east coast and had built up a solid reputation near the top 50 in both singles and doubles. He won five doubles titles, a discipline in which he reached the final of the 1987 Australian Open, then played on the grass he loved, with Laurie Warder.

I have particularly personal memories of Peter, which spanned 30 years, starting a couple of years after his defeat of Becker, when I bumped into him on a fairly empty tube train going from Queen's Club back to central London. Most international tennis stars would have (a) not been on the underground and (b) sniffed at an 11-stop conversation with a grubby 14-year-old, but Peter was a down-to-earth character, and he chatted to me all the way into town.

Almost 30 years later I managed to contact him again for a series I was writing for Wimbledon.com, and was particularly chuffed that he genuinely remembered our District Line journey from 1988. He was working in the States as a club pro and high-school coach, but took time out to chat at length about what he considered to be his small role in the Wimbledon story. Throughout the interview his humility shone through and his memory for detail was remarkable. This was best summed up when he recalled the short conversation he had at the net with Boris that day, 'Sorry about the record,' to which the German had replied, 'Don't worry, you were too good.' He remembered fondly how he would often chat to Boris at other events over the years, the two of them always making time for each other, bound together by history.

There was a civic reception in his hometown of Newcastle in NSW that summer of '87 and he was even given the keys to the city – the first sportsman to ever receive that honour. He played on for a few more years before eventually retiring in 1996, owner of an impressive career, boasting wins over Agassi, Mecir, Mayotte and Ivanisevic.

Peter and I stayed in contact, largely via email over the last few years, and it was with great sadness that I read his message to me detailing his battle with motor neurone disease and other associated complications, just before the 2017 Championships. He remained an admirable man to the end, both in the way he announced it to the world and in his refusal to feel sorry for himself or his situation. I spoke to him a month before he died and sent him the relevant extracts from this book. He sent an email back, saying that he had enjoyed the writing, adding, 'I'm very happy with my intro; folks might think what a bright fella I am!'

There was an awful lot more to Peter than that one victory, but for me he perfectly represents the beauty of this sport in the most simple of ways. On any given day, a player can achieve anything, wandering for no apparent reason in to the mythical field they call 'the zone', when everything just clicks. It is worth remembering him in that way, or even in the words of Boris himself, on that incredible day, when he touched the heights most of us can only dream of.

'I'm not immortal … it was like playing a man with a magic wand.'

ENDNOTES

I really like a footnote. My first book had a sizeable 228 which was met with both acclaim, 'Love the extra bits at the bottom' to disdain, 'This book is unreadable.' The first draft of this book had 347 footnotes, which was deemed excessive by the publishers. You could see their point. On researching the matter I discovered that David Foster Wallace's *Infinite Jest* is the standard bearer of the genre. In fact they are not footnotes, but endnotes, as they appear at the end of the book. His 1,079-page magnum opus contains a whopping 396 endnotes. Even some of the endnotes have their own endnotes. An impressive total of 96 pages of notes.

Whilst talking about my book in the same paragraph as a work by David Foster Wallace is cleverly upping its gravitas, I am writing only to let you know that I culled the number of footnotes to just 68, in order to increase enjoyment for the reader and be less of a self-indulgent prig. But these other little nuggets felt like gold to me, and I couldn't bear to just toss them in to cyber wasteland. So here are the best nuggets, which I simply couldn't bear to lose.

i.   As quoted on *Sue Barker: Our Wimbledon*, BBC One, 2017

ii.   Mikes, George, *How to be A Brit*, Penguin Books Reprint edition, London 2015

iii.   Mikes, George, *How to be A Brit*, Penguin Books Reprint edition, London 2015

iv.   JR Hartley was a charming fictional old gent who appeared in a Yellow Pages advert in the 80s, politely looking for an out-of-print book on fly fishing. It turned out that he was the author.

v.   Forbes, Gordon, *A Handful of Summers* (Heinemann, London 1978)

vi.   The *Daily Mirror* 29.6.84

vii.   Aaorangi Park was a former car park in the grounds which then became the site of the new No.1 Court. The area was leased to the New Zealand Sports & Social Club in the late 60s and the word 'Aorangi' means 'cloud in the sky', which is the Maori name for Mount Cook. Unlikely to ever come up in a pub quiz.

viii. The standing area was replaced in 1990 with seating. Not a commercial decision but the basic fact that the size of the arena meant that new rulings – linked to the Hillsborough and Bradford football tragedies – would not grant the court a safety certificate unless it was all-seater. As the AELTC themselves said, 'The place won't quite be the same without it.'

ix.   Anyone can apply to be an Honorary Steward, and they come from all walks of life with relevant backgrounds, such as the fire brigade. These men and women are also more than just a cosmetic presence. Unlike a bad barman who turns to face a busy crowd with the, 'Right, who's first?' approach – effectively asking us to do his job for him – the HS is all about taking the responsibility. They own that Queue and their presence is the cardinal reason why so many people love the whole experience.

x.   The *Daily Mail*, April 2016

xi.   French male players have continued to display this 'just happy to be here' attitude. They have become the masters of producing players who can reach the Top 50, even the Top 10, but seem happy to just get to the semis and leave it at that, not bothering to get their knees dirty with all that grubby winning stuff.

xii.   History is full of alliterative icons like Björn Borg and Boris Becker. See also Charlie Chaplin, Greta Garbo, Brigitte Bardot, Doris Day, Marilyn Monroe, Robert Redford, Sylvester Stallone, Tina Turner, Adam Ant and Fred Flintstone. I should really write a book, like a Malcolm Gladwell one, proving how people with alliterative names are more likely to succeed.

xiii. Iconic Aussie Roy Emerson was famed for embodying this spirit and establishing the 'no excuses' rule, saying: 'You should never complain about an injury. We believe that if you play, then you aren't injured, and that's that.'

xiv.   The *Daily Mirror* 27.6.87.

xv.   Martina Navratilova's record from 1982 to 1986, when she reached the final 78 times from 84 tournaments, will never be bettered.

xvi.   In his brilliant book *Ivan Lendl: The Man Who Made Murray*, Mark Hodgkinson describes this as 'treating Centre Court as a young child would a climbing frame.' The Club later installed a little gate to stop the necessity for clambering. Angry tweets saw a riot of terrible trash talking with 'Killjoy Gate' and 'Jobsworth Gate' only being topped by the mega-syllabled, 'Health-and-Safety-Gets-Out-of-Hand Gate'.

xvii.   A quote from Noel Gallagher, in reference to his brother, Liam.

xviii.   The *Daily Mirror* 24.6.88

xix.   The *Daily Mirror* and the Daily Express, respectively 2.7.88

xx.   *TODAY* 6.7.90

xxi.   Even earlier than that. Rumour was that Agassi had signed his first autograph aged six.

xxii.   Agassi skipped Wimbledon from his breakthrough year 1988 through to 1990, although he did actually play in 1987. He got hammered by French talent/joker/clown Henri Leconte in the first round.

xxiii.   The *Daily Telegraph* 24.6.91 and *The Sun* 28.6.91

xxiv.   *TODAY* and the *Daily Express*, respectively 25.6.92

xxv.   According to the *Daily Mail* 24.6.92

xxvi.   And McEnroe would have really loved that send-off. He always wanted so desperately to be liked, in his own weird way. Winning the doubles and a fair tilt at the singles. He topped his year by teaming up with Sampras and winning the Davis Cup Final doubles against Switzerland, alongside Agassi and Courier.

xxvii.   *The Sun* 29.6.93

xxviii.   *The Independent, The People* and the *News Of The World*, respectively 4.7.93.

xxix.   In 1981 *Sports Illustrated* reported that legendarily leggy Ginger Rogers had said that Hana Mandlikova had the most beautiful pins she had ever seen. This is not relevant, in any way, to the rest of this book.

xxx.   *Desert Island Discs* is a much loved, very old British radio show in which a well-known person is 'cast away' on a desert island and chooses their favourite tunes to accompany them in their lifelong solitude.

xxxi.   Ivanisevic hit 25 aces, taking his total for his tournament to 164, Sampras a meagre 17 to add to the 100 in his.

xxxii.   *The Independent* 25.6.96

xxxiii. Stripping Melissa was released by police without a caution. Cue lots of jokes about taking down her particulars. This was 1996, everything was fair game!

xxxiv. *The Sun* 3.7.97

xxxv. Becker's farewell was a reasonably big deal as Boris is so beloved in England, and the press gave him quite a send-off. AUF WIEDERSEHEN, NET said one desperate writer, HE'S OUR SUPER, SOARAWAY HUN, said another. 'I've felt at home here, I felt like I was one of them. They knew how to treat me...I'll miss them as much as they'll miss me hopefully,' Becker said on departure, and he could just as well have been talking about the country.

xxxvi. *The Sun* 23.6.98

xxxvii. The *Daily Mail* 22.6.98

xxxviii. *The People*, The *Sunday Mirror* and The *Sunday Telegraph*, respectively, 5.7.98

xxxix. *The Sun* 22.6.99

xl. The *Daily Mail* 1.7.99

xli. Tennis had a strange relationship with the girl who was named 'Martina' after the legend. Earlier in the summer at the French Open Final against Steffi Graf she had broken one of tennis's great rules when she walked round to Graf's side of the court to check a mark on a shot called out, which she thought was in. The Parisian crowd turned on her emphatically, not helped by a petulant Hingis serving underarm at one point. Graf took full advantage, leaving Hingis sobbing in defeat in her mother's arms. To absolutely no sympathy from the partisan crowd, chanting 'Steffi! Steffi!'

xlii. The *Daily Mirror* and *The Sun* 25.6.00

xliii. In 2015 I interviewed Björn Borg for a magazine in France. Never listen to people who say you should never meet your idols. Of course you should. If they turn out to shatter your dreams, get over it, not an idol any more. Björn Borg was an idol and was even more afterwards. I was greeted by a man who was exactly as you would imagine; calm, deep and considered. We went way over our allotted time and I came away not star struck but slightly humbled by someone who achieved so much, with such incredible grace and class, lost a lot of it, and then got it all back in spades.

xliv. *The Sun* 24.6.02

xlv. The *Daily Mirror* 25.6.02

xlvi. The *Player*, Boris Becker. Bantam, London: 2011

xlvii. The *Daily Mail* 5.7.04

xlviii. To quote John Lennon

xlix. The *Daily Mail* 20.06.05

l. The *Daily Mirror* 27.6.06

li.   Suzanne Lenglen was the first lady of women's tennis through the post-WW1 period, an uninhibited trailblazer and fashion icon. Legend has it that British-born designer Ted Tinling had ball-boyed for Lenglen on the Riviera, before going on to design beautiful tennis attire for women, including Gussie Moran's famous frilly knickers and Anne White's unitard.

lii.   *The Times* 04.07.06

liii.   Much like the fellas, very few Wimbledon Girls' champions go on to win the Ladies' title. At the time of writing only Martina Hingis and Amélie Mauresmo have achieved this.

liv.   *The Independent* 22.6.09

lv.   I actually wrote this down verbatim from the TV commentary. Unfortunately I have no idea who said it.

lvi.   The *Daily Mirror* 4.7.09

lvii.   The *News Of The World* 6.7.09

lviii.   The *Daily Mirror* 21.6.10

lix.   In the sage words of Alexander Pope.

lx.   *The Sun* 1.7.10

lxi.   *The Sun* 3.7.10

lxii.   In his 2012 detailed tennis study *Court Confidential* Neil Harman notes that a few years before, 'when asked whether Murray might be a contender one day, Federer dismissed that notion because he believed the Briton waited too long for the opponent to make a mistake.' He finished by saying, somewhat triumphantly, 'The lesson, Professor Federer, had been heeded.'

lxiii.   *The Sun* 5.7.13

lxiv.   As quoted on *Sue Barker: Our Wimbledon*, BBC One, 2017